The New Teacher's Survival Guide to Behaviour

Sue Roffey

Sue began her career as a teacher. She taught both in mainstream schools and in special provision for students with behavioural difficulty. She trained as an educational psychologist in 1987 and worked in London for many years. Sue completed her doctorate in 2000 and is now at the University of Western Sydney in Australia, specializing in behaviour and emotional literacy in education. She is the convenor for Emotional Literacy Australia (www.emotionalliteracy australia.com). Sue also provides international training and consultancy. This is her sixth book on issues related to behaviour in schools. Contact sue@suerof-fey.com.

The New Teacher's Survival Guide to Behaviour

Sue Roffey

P·C·P

Paul Chapman
Publishing

© Sue Roffey 2004
© Illustrations, Nic Watts 2004

First published 2004
Reprinted 2005, 2006, 2007

Paul Chapman Publishing
A SAGE Publications Company
1 Oliver's Yard
55 City Road
London EC1Y 1SP

SAGE Publications Inc
2455 Teller Road
Thousand Oaks, California 91320

SAGE Publications India Pvt Ltd
B 1/I 1 Mohan Cooperative Industrial Area
Mathura Road, New Delhi 110 044
India

SAGE Publications Asia-Pacific Pte Ltd
33 Pekin Street #02-01
Far East Square
Singapore 048763

Library of Congress Control Number: 2004104864

A Catalogue record for this book is available from the British
Library

ISBN 978-0-7619-4491-1
ISBN 978-0-7619-4492-8 (pbk)

Production by Deer Park Productions, Tavistock, Devon
Typeset by TW Typesetting, Plymouth, Devon
Printed in Great Britain by Cromwell Press, Trowbridge

Contents

Foreword

This book is much more than a 'survival' guide. Sue Roffey's tongue-in-cheek title both highlights the natural challenges in teaching yet provides the kind of skills and understandings that are essential to *be* a professional teacher.

From the outset Sue reminds us that teaching is much more than 'survival' more than 'coping'; it is a profession where individuals choose to make a difference in working with young people.

Based on sound research and wide experience in professional development this book provides accessible, realistic, honest and practical ways to address the natural challenges inherent in a multi-task profession like teaching.

Each chapter addresses an essential facet of the teaching profession: beginning with the individual – what it means '*being* a teacher' and then exploring teachers' values, and aims; how they build positive, respectful relationships with students, colleagues and their immediate parental community.

In each chapter there are essential skills that any new teacher will immediately benefit from. In particular the issue of challenging student behaviour is addressed with care to consider the total context of behaviour not only a teacher's immediate responses. Examples of how to manage and address student behaviour are given in every chapter particularly students with behaviour and learning needs.

One constant theme through the book is that of emotional 'literacy' and emotional intelligence: how we perceive and relate to others day-by-day – students, colleagues and parents. This is an essential feature of our relational and professional life as teachers and is addressed here with insight and relevance.

This book will encourage and reassure beginning teachers to be more aware of why they chose teaching; what its demands, challenges and joys are and will equip teachers to be more consciously and *professionally* self-aware in their role.

It is encouraging to affirm a book that celebrates that spending one's career working with, and for, young people is still meaningful, enjoyable and essential.

Bill Rogers

Acknowledgements

I would like to thank the following people, all of whom, in various ways, made important contributions to this book.

Louise Alfoura, Lucy Armstrong, Belinda Bayliss, Serena Carmel, Jale Dilek, Elizabeth Gillies, Robin Graeme-Holder, Gillian Lee, Michele Lindsay, Lyn Macpherson, Terry McKenzie, Emma Marshall, Maree Moir, Ann Rallison, Emily Rosen, Denise Sims and Ruth Sutton.

I am grateful also to all the teachers, students and other education professionals who shared their experiences.

Jude Bowen was the most supportive commissioning editor and David Roffey the most supportive partner I could wish for.

This book is dedicated to my wonderful daughter Emma, with thanks for the inspiration, the companionship and the coffee. Our stories are different; the message is the same.

Preface

Many new teachers go into their chosen profession with ideals, high hopes, energy and a determination to be effective facilitators of their students' learning. Research indicates that the majority of teachers entering the profession are highly motivated and dedicated to 'making a difference' in the world (Brighton, 1999). They begin by being more concerned with 'caring' than with 'discipline' (Weinstein, 1998), and more tuned into contributing to society than attaining a high wage (Wadsworth, 2001).

It is a tragedy for young people and for the future of society that so much dedication and enthusiasm is lost. The first few years can make or break a new teacher. It is estimated that over 20 per cent of teachers leave education in their first three years and up to 50 per cent within five years (Bobek, 2002; Currie, 2003; Patterson et al, 2003), with Australian, American, British and many other European figures mirroring each other. Forty per cent of trained teachers aged 25–29 in Australia are not working in the profession (Preston, 2000) with the greatest drop-out in the first year after training. Teacher retention is clearly a major concern throughout the developed world (Stoel and Thant, 2002).

The reasons given for this attrition include

- workload and the difficulties of juggling competing demands
- dealing with negativity
- teaching to test and other externally imposed objectives
- managing disruptive and disengaged students

- personal conflict in switching from being caring to being controlling

- lack of in-school support

- overwhelming in-school socio-political issues

- being unable to switch off at home.

The New Teacher's Survival Guide to Behaviour is aimed at improving teacher retention by suggesting a range of tools – behavioural, cognitive, affective and relational – which will enable new entrants to the profession to enjoy their work more. Although specifically addressing student behaviour, this book covers all aspects of the job that impinge on an individual teacher's ability to cope well in the classroom. It is anticipated that overall job satisfaction will be an outcome of feeling more effective, more supported, more aware of what makes a difference, and getting things into a perspective so that challenges are not overwhelming.

This book is based not so much on a list of strategies, but on fostering good practice and good relationships throughout the school. An eco-systemic perspective (Bronfenbrenner, 1979) asserts that events happen within embedded contexts which all influence each other. Neither a student's behaviour nor a teacher's behaviour happens in isolation. Both positive and negative scenarios are determined by the interaction of many factors. A single incident may have a trigger but it will also be the outcome of circular and cumulative causation. Not all of the contributing factors are, of course, within a new teacher's sphere of influence but it is important to understand what they are and what can be changed. Specific approaches by individuals can and do make small differences quickly and, if applied consistently, can make big changes over time.

This book therefore begins with a focus on the individual teacher both as a person and within their new role. It proceeds to look at interactions within the class, followed by the school system and the community the school serves. The wider socio-political system, although crucially important, is not within our scope here.

Within each chapter the focus is on issues related to behaviour from a wide range of angles. We specifically explore perspectives on the following.

- Minimizing stressful scenarios in the first place by
    - identifying what teachers need
    - identifying what effective teachers do
    - clarifying expectations for work and behaviour
    - engaging with students in ways which maximize mutual respect
    - being authoritative rather than authoritarian
    - communicating confidence
    - promoting positive behaviour
    - nipping potential disruption in the bud
    - avoiding the battleground scenario
    - focusing on the positive and the possible
    - listening out for constructive discourse in the staffroom
    - identifying support – from policies to people
    - maximizing resources, including emotional energy
    - looking at time management.
- Dealing with difficulties that arise by
    - examining what difficult behaviour represents
    - working with the whole person rather than just the problem
    - avoiding labelling, negativity and destructive discourse
    - solution-focused approaches
    - responding to challenges in emotionally intelligent ways
    - knowing what it is appropriate and possible to change and what it is not
    - seeking active support

- working most effectively with parents, carers and the community
- de-escalating confrontations.
- The aftermath
  - maintaining dignity and integrity when all else fails
  - what helps in picking yourself up and starting over?
  - getting things into perspective.

The New Teacher's Survival Guide is about how teachers think about themselves and the students they teach. This includes their understanding of what their job entails, the role they are in, how they think about their students, the expectations they have and the relationships they develop. It includes how both personal and social constructs underpin ways of being in the classroom that either help individual teachers survive or pull them under. It is also about ensuring that teacher survival is not at the expense of students nor gained by compromising beliefs about best practice in the face of crises and demands.

Chapter 1

Introduction

BEING A TEACHER

Being a teacher is potentially a meaningful, rewarding and stimulating profession. Spending time with young people, from little children to teenagers, can be both fascinating and fun. This book has been written so that you, as a new teacher, might have the best possible chance of having a good time at work; enough of a good time to want to stay in education, motivated, fully involved and passionate about the difference you can make to your students and their future.

A 'good time' is defined as a sense of self-efficacy and job satisfaction. It is not about getting away with the minimum effort but making your efforts worthwhile. It is not about ducking difficulties but exploring ways of facing them so they do not overwhelm you.

Here you will find suggestions about ways of being in school that enable you to enjoy the interaction both with the students you teach and also with colleagues who support you. This includes

- getting and maintaining credibility in your new role

- putting respect into operation

- developing student self-awareness and self-control

- dealing with conflict and confrontation in ways which do not undermine your sense of self and purpose

- seeing difficulties as part of the challenge, not the reason to fear coming through the school gates.

DON'T DREAD MONDAYS

The Sunday sinking sensation! Anyone who has been in education has been there. The grabbing of those last few moments of weekend indulgence before the anxiety of the next day takes hold. There are some teachers, however, who seem to survive and thrive because they love what they are doing. This book will help you become one of the few – and should the few become the many we will have education itself transformed!

There will inevitably be days which are more stressful than others, that's life – but the aim here is to maximize and maintain that sense of purpose, fun and commitment with which most people enter the profession. This is not only about not dreading Mondays but actively looking forward to the whole of your working week!

WAYS OF SEEING THE WORLD

This book encourages you to be aware of how you think about things. Note how a group of teachers talk about their job, the classes they teach, families, individual students and their colleagues. This discourse presents a way of being – it constructs what is seen as the 'truth' without acknowledging that it is, in fact, only one version of several possible 'truths'. Other teachers may have different ways of talking about the same things.

For instance, a teenager who is described as insolent, disruptive and 'conduct disordered' is one version of the 'reality' of that young person. He is clearly viewed as a problem. A teenager who is said to be struggling to cope with his feelings of rejection and inability to read and doing so in ways that might make sense to him but seem irrational to teachers is another version. This same student is seen to be having problems rather than being a problem. The teacher who is exploring what is possible to change to maximize the chance of that young person being more settled and learning effectively in school has yet another interpretation of the situation. Sometimes problems are seen only in the light of what is seen as 'normal' and there are vested interests in determining what that might be. We analyse what are useful ways of thinking and how these can impact both on what you do in school and how you feel about being there.

YOUR FIRST TIME

The first time you go into school as a newly qualified teacher may be nerve racking. First of all you have to negotiate the staffroom; find out where it is, check which mug it is acceptable to fill with coffee and where to sit so as not to offend anyone. And you haven't come anywhere near the students yet!

Over the next few weeks you get to know the ropes – what is supposed to happen and what really goes on. You find out what is valued and what is not, what is seen as important in the school and what is important outside the school, what the pressures are and staff responses to these. You work out the expectations and start to think about how you are going to meet them. It is exciting but also scary.

YOU AS A TEACHER AND YOU AS A PERSON

For the past few years you have been in the role of student yourself. Now you have a very different role, the teacher role. What does this mean and how do you take on this new way of being in the world?

This book is about you: you in your new role, you as a complex person with strengths, limitations and needs – just like your students. It is about the way you think of yourself, the way you think of the children and young people you teach and how you build the relationships you need to have. You have exactly the same issues as the students in many ways – pressure to 'perform', issues of control, how to get the maximum amount of satisfaction out of your days, and how to make experiences meaningful and worthwhile.

People will give you lots of advice and it's hard to know which to follow and which to discard. Knowing yourself and your values will help you in making the dozens of daily decisions that come your way. Hold onto the fact that although you are no longer a student you are still a learner and that mistakes are part of the learning process. Don't lose sleep over not getting it exactly right all the time.

You need to look after yourself well to maximize your chances of survival in the classroom. Your physical and emotional well-being is an integral part of who you are and how you function. Chapter 3: You and Your Resources explores how you maintain a high level of personal resources and also how to manage your precious time.

THE SCHOOL YOU ARE IN

Over the first few days and weeks you will gather information about the ethos of the school and who and what is maintaining the current culture – otherwise known as 'the way things happen around here'. There are other clues to this: what is on the walls, how students are spoken to, how staff speak to each other and about each other. You may find a staffroom of deep demoralization or one of enthusiastic creativity. In some schools everyone takes responsibility for what happens, in other schools it seems that no-one does. The conversations in these schools usually go along the lines 'everything is awful and it's all someone else's fault!' Most schools are somewhere in between and you will need to think about where you fit in and feel most comfortable. Stand back and see if you can evaluate elements of the ethos and how that culture is being maintained.

THE STUDENTS YOU TEACH

During these first few weeks you are also negotiating your place as the teacher in the classroom. Your students will try to work out what you are like and how you will teach. They will test out their relationship with you and see how you respond to some of the things they do. They will work out how much you tune into them and whether you teach in ways that engage their interest. They will be fascinated by how you manage students who are more challenging and here they will be looking for personal qualities of self-control and self-respect, humour, enthusiasm and confidence. If you are prone to losing your temper you will be giving them an excellent diversionary side-show so some bright sparks will be seeing if you are going to be an entertainer they can wind up to perform.

This book is about the package of survival skills you need to thrive. And nearly all those skills are linked to relationships. A strategy is only as good as the context in which it is embedded – and the most powerful aspect of context is relationship. There is a good deal of research to confirm that the establishment and maintenance of classroom discipline is linked to intra and interpersonal competencies. This, in brief, is how well you understand yourself and how well you get on with others. Research shows that this includes your relationship with pupils (Oberski et al, 1999; Stuhlman and Pianta, 2002), colleagues (Hall et al, 1997), significant others, such as parents, partners and friends (Cairns and Brown, 1998; Miller, 2003) and yourself (Hertzog, 2002).

Students are more likely to behave well if the relationship you have with them is based on fairness, negotiation and mutual respect. That takes time to build, so how do you react in those first few days and how do you plan to establish your own culture of how things will happen in your classroom? How you present yourself initially to the students needs to be the foundation for this development.

YOUR GREATEST CHALLENGES

It will be tempting for busy new teachers to wait until they get into hot water, then jump to Chapter 7: You and Your Biggest Challenges to find out what they might have done! Please take the time to at least skim the whole book. Perhaps highlight ways of working that make sense to you. The search for quick fix solutions plagues our society and education is not exempt. There is not a simple, single strategy that will ensure your survival and help you thrive in the classroom. It is the whole package that makes a difference.

You can pick up a strategy and carry it into the classroom with you but how well it works depends on the context in which you attempt to put it into operation. It's a bit like trying to watch a video or DVD when your player doesn't work properly. Most of this book is about the construction of the optimal context to ensure that your strategies work well at the point of challenge in the classroom.

Chapter 7 looks at different ways of thinking about children who challenge and actions you might take on the basis of these constructs. It helps you to separate out what you do to deal with difficult behaviour from what you might do in the longer term. Strategies that only deal with immediate management are exhausting because you have to keep doing them. This chapter addresses some of the more challenging situations you might come across in the classroom and provides you with a repertoire of ideas to respond most effectively. This in itself will make you feel more in control.

Finally we look at what you need to survive on the worst of days when nothing seems to work and your self-esteem is under the carpet. What do you need to do to pull yourself up and out to face another day and another class?

THE BASIS OF SURVIVAL

This guide has developed from a number of strands. It is based on the following ideas.

- Eco-systemic thinking – everything is connected and mutually influential.

- Social constructionist perspectives in critical psychology – there is more than one version of a 'truth' and different realities are constructed by how things are presented and discussed. The powerful have an interest in determining which 'truths' get to be dominant.

- Personal construct psychology – we all try to make sense of the world and what happens to us: experiences, expectations and interpretations are circular.

- Other psychological perspectives with regard to development, learning and behaviour.

- Educational research on teacher attrition.

- Educational research on school culture and ethos.

- Educational and psychological research on the promotion of positive behaviour and management of challenging behaviour.

- The developing knowledge base in the field of emotional literacy.

- Specific research on new teachers and behaviour.

- The author's interpretations of her experience from the varying perspectives of student, teacher, educational psychologist, academic and parent.

This book presents a somewhat different view of a teacher's experience in a school. It is about conceptualization more than strategies, interaction as much as curriculum, pre-requisites for learning as well as pedagogical style. In taking this direction it tries not to duck issues that really matter. The frameworks are about the negotiation of power and control that meets the needs of everyone as much as possible. An optimal classroom ethos needs the development of emotionally literate interactions – ones that are assertive without being aggressive, that acknowledge and take account of the affective and that allow you to maintain personal integrity in the face of opposition – whether that is from students, parents or colleagues.

YOU CAN DO IT!

This is the way it is – this is the way to survive. There are other ways too – but those are not the ways of the emotionally and strategically fittest. Some teachers see survival as the need to win an inevitable battle for control of the classroom and others become bedded down somewhere quiet just getting through the days and waiting for the rescue of retirement. Don't do this – the next generation needs you! They need you engaged, active, interested, empathic, self-aware and interpersonally skilled. You can do it – with help. Here's a start.

Chapter 2

You as a Teacher

Remember what the flight attendant says in the safety talk before your plane takes off? 'Put your own oxygen mask on first and then help others.' Here you have a chance to check out your values, motivations, perceptions and basic emotional literacy. The better you understand yourself and how you respond to the world around you, the more able you will be to reflect on the decisions you make and the actions you take. This gives you more choices in the way you approach your work. This chapter helps identify your skills and strengths and what you need to develop. You may find that, in order to maximize your chances of surviving, you need to increase your personal resources in some way or perhaps think a little differently about your role or the students you teach.

The first section focuses on understanding yourself, the way you think and feel. We then explore what it means to become a teacher and what basic skills you need to fulfil the role well. This is not about knowledge of the job or your subject, but knowledge of how to present yourself to your students so that you have maximum credibility. You are shown how to look calm, confident and in control even if you have to begin by putting on an act! There are also thoughts on avoiding some basic pitfalls.

YOU AS A PERSON

Why did you become a teacher?

People become teachers for many reasons, most of them intrinsic. Few do it for the money! Many go into teaching because they had a great time at school: they were successful and by and large teachers liked them. They decided this was the career for them before they left school themselves. A few others have the opposite reason. They managed to survive the experience, but it wasn't really enjoyable. They reckon they can do a better job than their own teachers did. Sometimes they had a really miserable time and go into teaching passionate about giving their students a fair deal, especially standing up for those who are disadvantaged.

Most beginning teachers are full of ideals, they want to make a difference (Wadsworth, 2001). They are often caring and concerned about social justice – really nice people. One of the reasons teachers leave is that they feel these values are just not given an airing. They become disillusioned and find themselves behaving in ways that are not congruent with their beliefs (Weinstein, 1998). Instead of being someone who cares they find themselves becoming someone who controls. Sometimes this is to do with the students, sometimes it is to do with the school and its ethos and sometimes with the 'system' – the organization, bureaucracy and structures that permeate everyday life and dictate what is and is not possible. All of these interrelate and influence each other. What is addressed here is how to maintain the role of a caring teacher whilst promoting a learning environment that fosters a sense of order, purpose and behaviour appropriate for school: the two are not mutually exclusive.

The rationale behind your decision to enter the teaching profession will have an impact on how you see yourself in the role, how you think about your students, colleagues and parents, and how vulnerable you are to stress and/or disillusionment.

Which of the following statements relate to your motivation to teach?

- Education is a way of making the world a better place.
- I just love my subject.
- Teaching is a job where I can make a difference.
- I've always wanted to be a teacher.

- Members of my family are teachers – it's what I know.
- People admire and respect teachers.
- I enjoy being with kids.
- I'm a bit of a kid myself!
- I prefer working with children.
- I am a good communicator.
- I want an outlet for all my creativity.
- I'm well organized and confident I will be good at it.
- I love a challenge!
- The hours and holidays are good.
- It will fit in with family commitments.
- It's a regular job with a regular income.
- You can teach anywhere.
- I couldn't think of anything else to do.
- Something else motivated me.

All of these motivations have a potentially positive and negative aspect. People who became teachers because they couldn't think of anything else to do might find it is their vocation after all. Having no expectations might result in less disappointment. Teachers who are just like kids themselves may relate brilliantly on one level but have a struggle when it comes to necessary classroom management. Those who are in teaching for the long holidays may be more balanced in their outlook on life, but will have to look carefully at their commitment during term time in order to do a good job. Good communicators may be great talkers but need to learn to listen. Think about why *you* went into teaching and how this understanding can work for you and what difficulties it might present.

There are, however, two motivations that are especially helpful in the classroom. Students are more likely respond well to your teaching if you have a passion for what you do – especially if you are skilled in communicating your enthusiasm. The other important motivation is a genuine interest in the students – liking children and wanting to make a difference. Empathy shows and it matters (Roffey et al, 2004).

Values – what is important to you?

Your values are part of your identity. We can become defensive when someone challenges our core beliefs about how the world should be. Clarifying your values will help you understand why you respond in certain ways to events. Sometimes we take on values without thinking much about them and their implications, and sometimes we impose our values on other people without realizing what this might mean.

The education system in the West is an example of a clash of values. We live in a society that values individuality, autonomy and self-determination, but expects our citizens – especially our students – to do as they are told (Elliott, 2004). We want them to cooperate whilst at the same time being in competition with each other. Freedom is undoubtedly valuable, but one person's individual freedom may disadvantage others. Laws impose limits on freedom and few would argue with that. There are shadows as well as ideals in the values we hold and we need to be aware of both. No-one is value free. The following exercise is not intended to throw your central beliefs into doubt but to provide an opportunity for you to reflect upon them, how they came about and which may be helpful and congruent with your role as a teacher.

Reflection point

List the five things that matter most to you.

List the five things you would most like to change about the world.

List the five things you hope to achieve in the next ten years.

- Where do these values come from?

- What do they say about you as a new teacher?

- What will be helpful and less helpful to you in practice?

- Can you identify anything that might cause you conflict or challenge?

- Will you try to put these values into practice in the classroom?

- How might you do that while respecting that different things may be important to some of your students and others in the school?

Personal and professional integrity comes from being consistent in putting your values into operation. Sometimes expedience seems an easier option, but you will lose credibility if you say one thing and do another.

Avoiding disillusionment

The very values that make the most caring and conscientious teachers are those that might lead to the greatest disillusionment. Most educators say it is the constant niggles that wear them down rather than major incidents in the classroom (DfES, 1989; Hastings and Bham, 2003). Although some schools have high levels of violence these are comparatively rare: a report in the US (Cantor and Wright, 2002) determined that over 60 per cent of violent incidents happen in 4 per cent of high schools. The behaviours that drain emotional resources, especially from concerned and sympathetic teachers, are those that demonstrate a lack empathy, or values that see denial and dishonesty as useful. This is especially true in high schools where patterns of behaviour have become ingrained – it is often hard to see the needy individual under the bravado and the foul language.

In the UK, schools for students with emotional and behavioural difficulties were once called schools for 'maladjusted' children. It is more pertinent to view pupils as adjusting in the best way they know to situations in their lives. It makes a difference how you think about students. Construing behaviour as a way of making sense of the world provides a different dimension. This may enable you to work more effectively with those young people who appear to hold none of the values that are important to you. Closer investigation may, however, uncover values that are not all anti-social. These may only apply to elements of a person's life but there may be foundations to build upon.

Craig had a reputation for being a 'hard case'. He was quick to throw his weight around and was verbally abusive to both teachers and other students. He had a very short fuse and had been suspended from school several times. Craig also had a little sister, twelve years his junior. In Craig's eyes, she could do no wrong. He allowed her to use his things, mess up his room and eat his chocolate. He taught her every swear word he knew and she kept him constantly delighted by repeating these forbidden phrases! She adored her big brother, was probably the one person in his world who ever did – and he repaid her in full with loyalty, kindness, generosity and affection.

In the unlikeliest places you may find values you can share – but you might have to dig deep.

EMOTIONAL LITERACY – HOW WELL DO YOU UNDERSTAND WHAT YOU FEEL?

Emotional literacy comprises

- awareness of and reflection on your own feelings
- skills relating to emotional regulation
- having a repertoire of appropriate emotional expression
- being able to tune effectively into others
- skills in emotionally charged situations
- maintaining a positive and optimistic outlook.

These skills can be learnt and practised. We can identify factors that promote the development of emotionally literate classrooms and schools (Antidote, 2003) as well as emotionally and socially competent individuals (Weare, 2003).

Behavioural issues in schools are steeped in emotion. We talk about how students' feelings are expressed but less often, and certainly less overtly, about teachers. How well adults understand and manage their own feelings has an impact on what they do and how they handle situations. The most appropriate and helpful ways of responding to distressed children are those of emotionally aware and skilled teachers. This does not mean ignoring feelings or being bland but communicating in ways that are most effective. There is more on this in Chapter 7: You and Your Biggest Challenges. Emotionally literate teachers are also able to stay positive and resilient because they optimize their emotional resources (see Chapter 3: You and Your Resources).

Check out your own emotional literacy. Your values, thoughts and emotions are not separate but part of each other. If you come from a background where high achievement is valued you might feel you must do everything to the highest possible standard. If approval from your line managers is not forthcoming you may feel miserable. If your family values loyalty rather than attainment your feelings will be different. The emotions we experience are often socially constructed: we are embarrassed because we have broken social codes in some way and are similarly proud when we achieve something that our culture has determined is valuable. This doesn't mean that the feelings don't exist, but that they can change when we have new information or develop different beliefs. We may, for instance, believe that people with a certain appearance are more likely to be terrorists. This may make us feel less well disposed towards individuals in our community and our behaviour less friendly. Once we get to know these people as part of a hard working family our beliefs about them change and we become less wary. If staffroom conversation leads you to believe that a student is 'nothing but trouble' your feelings and actions may be negative until you find out more about the circumstances.

Emotional awareness

Do you know what your emotional 'triggers' are: the things that easily make you embarrassed, angry, ashamed, anxious, defensive or otherwise upset? Some individuals may be sensitive to the way they look, others are more anxious about being seen as competent. Many teachers have strong responses to the way some pupils treat others. Students may tune into these triggers and see if they can wind you up. Be prepared (see Chapter 7).

According to Goleman (1995) some of our emotional triggers are related to pre-verbal emotional memory about what happened to us as infants. We may be taken by surprise by how strongly we feel about something. An emotionally literate response does not allow this trigger to result in a destructive explosion.

Most teachers find it hard not to take things personally. In most cases a student will be bringing emotions that have little to do with what is happening in your class but school might be the safer place to let them rip.

14-year-old Bryn started on the younger kids as soon as he came in the door, swearing and kicking the furniture. When the teacher approached he turned his attention to her, telling her what he thought of her in no uncertain terms. It would be understandable if the teacher reacted angrily, taking this verbal assault personally. She realized, however, that he could not be angry with her as he had only just come into school and she hadn't done anything to him – yet! He was allowed to calm down in the office where it transpired that his father, who now lived with a new family in another part of the country, had promised to phone that weekend. Bryn had waited at home for the call, which never came. He was beside himself with anger and hurt. It was easier to rage than to cry – though the tears did eventually come. A teacher who felt she had a right to respond with anger would have missed the reality for this student. As it was Bryn's teacher was able to validate his feelings but also eventually talk to him about ways of expressing anger differently.

Emotional regulation

This is about finding ways to feel better, calmer and more in control. Although easier said than done it can be learnt and practised. Buddhist monks are skilled in distancing themselves from negative emotions and reducing all the associated physical sensations by transforming their thinking (Goleman, 2003). Emotions are often generated by negative voices in our head telling us we are not good enough or no-one likes us. Some inner voices are more aggressive, such as, 'get one over on him', 'get your own back', 'she deserves what she's getting'. Emotional regulation is about ways of feeling calmer and constructive. Do you know what is helpful to you?

Emotional expression

We are entitled to our feelings but need to take responsibility for the way these are expressed. Anger itself is not necessarily a problem and has been the motivator for many social advances. Sometimes anger comes at us from out of left field and many believe we have a right to take it out on the person who appears to have triggered it. This exacerbates situations. Teachers who shriek at students because they have had enough invariably make things worse. Labelling, finger pointing, sarcasm and shouting are all responses that undermine relationships and model inappropriate behaviour. Stating firmly but calmly that the triggering behaviour is unacceptable and has consequences is a strong response that is less likely to have unwanted repercussions. Using statements that acknowledge feelings related to behavioural triggers but do not start with 'you are . . .' or 'you make me . . .' are easier for students to hear and less damaging to relationships. Always refer to behaviour, not to the student. For example, 'That behaviour is not acceptable in this class, I understand that you are unhappy with the decision however it is now time to take out your books.' Words and phrases that work for you and your students are best thought out and rehearsed before you need them. You will be less likely to revert to words that you might regret later if you have considered some useful phrases in advance (see 'De-escalating confrontations' in Chapter 7).

CHANGING ROLE

You are about to take on a very different role from the one you may have been in for several years. This means that there will be new expectations of you and you will develop new ways of seeing yourself. For many the transition is smooth but others find it harder to relinquish being a student.

The student role implies being a learner, being directed, and having individual responsibility for your own work but not for anyone else. The role of the teacher is one of authority. It is the teacher who determines the content and process of lessons, awards marks and is responsible for all the students. It is your role to be the director of proceedings – do not relinquish this. Many of the ideas given in Chapter 4: You and Your Class show how to stay in charge while giving students choices and freedoms within your given framework.

Part of your role as a new teacher may come as a surprise. You are the newcomer, the least experienced, and in some more hierarchical school systems you are therefore on the lowest rung. As a student you may have been expected to question and initiate. This might not be valued in your school and you will struggle with the balance of now being an authority with the students but with little power in the system. Look for where it is acceptable to ask questions and be innovative.

BEING FRIENDLY – NOT A FRIEND

The chances are that you may not be much older than your students. You may share their tastes in music, clothes, films and sport. It is tempting to want to be seen as 'one of the crowd'. This is not appropriate and will interfere with your personal credibility when it comes to any showdown. Think about boundaries and what would be considered a mature response in any interaction. Talking about a film, gig or match is fine but sharing tales about your wild Saturday night or swearing about the opposing team gives an entirely different impression. Keeping a certain distance while still being friendly and approachable will be to your advantage – being over familiar might rebound on you.

PERSONAL QUALITIES YOU NEED FOR SURVIVAL

Self-respect

Think of the people for whom you have a high level of respect. You will find that those you admire behave as if they believe they are worthwhile without being brash. They are able to celebrate the success of others because they do not need to focus on themselves. They manifest self-respect. It is the same in the classroom. Students respond better to adults who behave with self-respect. They respond less well to those who present themselves as timid and self-deprecating and also give short shrift to those who are full of themselves without the accompanying competence.

So what does self-respect look like in practice?

- I believe that I am a capable person even though I might make mistakes sometimes.

- I am ready to have a go at things.

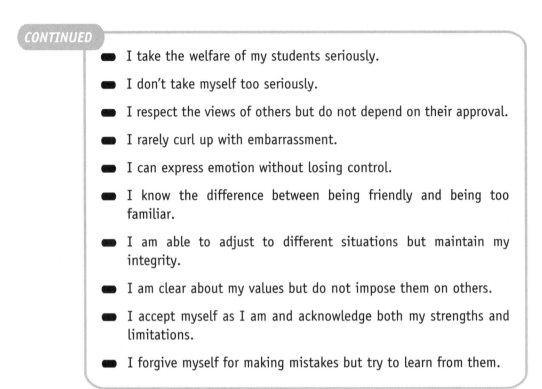

CONTINUED

- I take the welfare of my students seriously.

- I don't take myself too seriously.

- I respect the views of others but do not depend on their approval.

- I rarely curl up with embarrassment.

- I can express emotion without losing control.

- I know the difference between being friendly and being too familiar.

- I am able to adjust to different situations but maintain my integrity.

- I am clear about my values but do not impose them on others.

- I accept myself as I am and acknowledge both my strengths and limitations.

- I forgive myself for making mistakes but try to learn from them.

Confidence

Even people with self-respect may find new situations daunting. It is hard to behave with confidence when you are a bundle of nerves. How you present yourself to your new class, however, is a loud message about how you rate yourself. Creeping around with your head down does you no favours. It says you are a potential target or victim. Even if you do feel like shaking in your shoes, don't let the students see! Behaving with confidence is one of the most important things you can do in your first few weeks, and then it becomes second nature. This is how you do it!

Body language

Practise confident body language. Keep yourself upright but not defensive or rigid. A relaxed posture works well but try to stay symmetrical. Leaning to one side can give an impression of lethargy rather than alert relaxation. People who take courses in giving presentations are told that 'four square' matters. This means having your feet in line with your shoulders and keeping your hands out of your pockets. Avoid pointing fingers (accusatory), crossing your arms over your chest (defensive), putting your hands on your hips (aggressive) of jangling keys or coins in your pocket (nervous and distracted).

Walk around the place as if you know what you are about. If you really don't know where you are going, ask a student rather than peer around corners or wait for them to notice you are lost. Even better, get hold of a map of the layout, especially for a big school.

⬤ Voice

Teachers who are having a hard time often talk too fast. Slowing down your delivery pays dividends in several ways. It makes you seem more in control of the situation and should help with fluency. Too many hesitations interrupt the flow of communication and interfere with the transfer of meaning. It is hard to concentrate on an erratic delivery.

Some teachers will tell you that you have to shout. Except in very exceptional circumstances there are better and more effective ways of getting attention (see Chapter 4). Drop the volume of your voice and keep the pitch low rather than high. Squeaky high tones sound more nervous and uncertain.

⬤ Facial expression

Our faces are the mirror to our minds. We deliver powerful messages by the expressions that are on them. If you are thinking, 'This child is the nastiest piece of work I have come across, get me out of here', the chances are that your cheek muscles will tighten, your mouth turn down and your eyes go cold! The key to having positive facial expressions is to keep some positive thoughts wherever possible. Try alternatives such as, 'this child must have had a hard time to be like this' or if this is one step too far try, 'if I get through the next half hour I deserve chocolate'! Your facial expression will therefore be one of hopefulness rather than condemnation or fear.

⬤ Eye contact

The importance of good eye contact cannot be over estimated. With smaller children, get down to their level to interact with them and maximize eye contact. Do not demand that they look back directly at you. In some cultures this is not considered polite and for some shy children it's just excruciating. It is what *you* do that matters. Smile readily but not rigidly when you make eye contact.

All of these things say 'I'm OK, how are you?' Positive body language will also make you feel better about yourself and the day you are having. You don't only smile when you feel good – you feel good when you smile. The same applies to walking tall (Laird and Apostoleris, 1996).

BEWARE THE OBVIOUS – AVOID DISTRACTIONS

With the most emotionally literate approach, the greatest confidence in the world and the best-prepared lessons you can come unstuck on some basics. No-one will mention these unmentionables to you but each of them can undermine your personal authority. Of course, you have a right to be yourself and express your individuality. The choices you make, however, will impact in ways you may not want.

The first is personal hygiene. You may be blissfully unaware of body odour, bad breath, stale cigarette smoke, alcohol fumes and pet animal smells on your clothes but your students will notice. It does not help your credibility as a dynamic teacher if there is evidence that you cannot look after yourself properly.

The second is bare flesh or outrageous fashion. You may think that you have a great body and are proud of displaying your bare midriff to anyone. You may also believe it will help your relationship with students if you keep up with the latest fashion. The following outcomes, however, are not helpful to you as a teacher.

- It sets you up in potential competition with students.

- It may stimulate powerful adolescent fantasies.

- It may be disrespectful to the cultural norms of the community; you may offend families – and this means putting up barriers to working with them.

If everyone, staff and students, sports a nose ring you won't stand out by having one too – but if it is a minority fashion maybe you could put it in when you get home. Extreme statements in the classroom are not a good idea.

The third is awareness of touch. There are now guidelines in all education systems about not touching students. Make yourself aware of them. The occasional brief hand on the forearm in an empathic or congratulatory gesture is probably not going to be a problem but do not risk getting a reputation as someone who cannot keep their hands to themselves. At best students may consider it an intrusion on their privacy, at worst you could be up for harassment. If you are teaching small children they may sometimes come up to you for a reassuring hug. It is damaging to turn them away if they are in need but do this in full view of others and make it appropriately brief. For your own security avoid seeing children on their own in places where there is no visible access to a public thoroughfare. Keep doors open.

APPROPRIATE ASSERTIVENESS

This combines issues of confidence, self-respect and emotional literacy.

There are three ways of responding in challenging or upsetting situations.

- The mouse position in which you buckle under and stay silent, probably giving yourself an ulcer as well as a bad attack of low-self esteem; all your energy is put into ducking the issue and rationalizing why you have opted out.

- The aggressive response or fight mechanism – usually this means a knee jerk reaction and attacking back; this can set a pattern in which the stakes simply get higher – it rarely has a positive outcome for anyone.

- The flow response, otherwise known as appropriate assertiveness; the suggestions in Chapters 4 and 7 promote this mode.

Appropriate assertiveness is stating what has happened, your response and what you want or need – for example, 'When you are shouting at me, I cannot hear what you want to say. I need you to calm down a bit'. The initial statement needs to be as objective as possible without loaded phrases: 'when you don't tidy up . . .' is better than 'when you just walk off and leave this room like a pig-sty . . .'. Avoid putting interpretations on someone's behaviour and assuming motivation or intent. State what has happened as simply as possible.

Your response can be an action or feeling: 'when you talk all through the lesson I'm not going to make the effort to make it interesting next time/I feel really angry and fed up'. Using 'I' statements reduces the placing of blame. This gives resolution a greater chance of working. The final statement is what you want to happen. It is useful to provide an element of choice rather than be didactic. Anything giving the message 'you have got to' is likely to be met with resistance. Keeping to 'I' statements also helps with reaching resolutions: 'I would value some help here'.

You won't always get what you need or want by being appropriately assertive but it has a much better chance than the other two options. You also feel better about yourself.

SUMMARY

This chapter has explored what it means to become a teacher, and the values, motivations and skills you bring with you. All of these impact on how you do the job, how you think about students and how you respond to difficulties. Important things to develop are confidence and emotional literacy.

Chapter 3

You and Your Resources

The previous chapter helped identify the personal attributes and qualities that impinge on your role as a teacher. This chapter focuses on your personal resources and how to maximize these so you stay on top of the job.

A certain level of stress is not necessarily a bad thing. It can be motivating, energizing and productive. Stress only becomes a problem when demands exceed the resources to meet them. Teaching takes a lot out of you. It makes demands on your time, physical energy, creativity, the ability to think on your feet and on your emotional resources. You will be more able to respond thoughtfully and effectively to challenges in the classroom if your own resources are kept topped up. The best laid plans, good intentions and positive relationships will melt away like snowballs in a heat wave if you are feeling so stressed that all you can manage is knee jerk reactions. Such reactions usually exacerbate difficulties and may set you up for negative expectations in the future. This chapter looks at ways to keep demands within sensible boundaries and how to identify and maximize your available resources so as to remain on an even keel. On the surface it might seem that your life outside school has nothing to do with how effectively you respond to student behaviour. In reality it has everything to do with your survival in challenging circumstances. The same principles, by the way, are also true of your students.

It is now widely accepted that there are strong links between physical and psychological well-being. You are more likely to become ill if you find your working environment emotionally stressful and to be emotionally drained if you are feeling tired and under par. You need to give yourself every chance to develop optimum resilience.

PHYSICAL RESOURCES

You have a better chance of getting through the day, and especially facing a hard class if you look after yourself well. Good quality sleep, keeping healthy, and time for relaxation all make a difference to your survival in school.

Staying healthy

Everyone gets sick from time to time, but giving your immune system a better chance can boost resilience to illness. Some people are lucky enough to have an iron constitution but we can all maximize our optimum levels of fitness and energy. Trying to give a stimulating lesson when you feel like death warmed up is very difficult. Taking lots of time off with colds and viruses at best prevents your becoming established and at worst risks your credibility.

The following are the fundamentals of good physical health.

Good quality sleep   Being tired makes people irritable, impulsive and less able to think strategically – a devastating combination when working with challenging students. Stay up all night at the weekend if you like but get the sleep you need during the week. If you have a young family who keep you up at night organize all the support you can.

If you have a head full of the 'to do' list, getting to sleep and staying asleep might be difficult. Stop thinking about work at least an hour before bedtime. Relax with whatever works for you, a non-caffeine drink, warm bath, walking the dog, riveting book, sex!

If your brain goes into overdrive the minute your head hits the pillow, make a conscious effort to focus on your achievements rather than things there are still to do. If none of this works, learn relaxation or meditation techniques. These can be very effective.

If you have been drinking alcohol, drink plenty of water before you turn off the light, this will help stop you waking up at night with a raging thirst and a headache.

Sleep is part of your time management. It is easy to say to yourself that you can plan for Monday's class after the last program on television on Sunday night. Well, you can, but what is your delivery going to be like?

Eating well   Start the day with your blood sugar levels up so you have your body and brain in gear. This means having breakfast. Something that releases energy slowly during the morning is best – like a cooked breakfast. A cup of black coffee won't meet your needs but a piece of fruit or a slice of toast, even on the run, is better than nothing. At the very least put one of those muesli bars in your pocket so you can snack at the traffic lights. Just don't try and get to break time with no energy boost. At lunchtime take the break you are entitled to – it is as important as the food you eat. There is plenty of information available about good diet. You will know what that is, lots of fresh produce, good levels of protein and not too much fat or sugar. You will also know that eating too little or too much slows you down and depletes your precious energy. Drinking lots of water is a good idea as it helps flush toxins out of your system.

Taking regular exercise   Easier said than done when you are busy and everything else seems a priority. Choose something active you enjoy and do it as regularly as you can manage. This could be anything from walking to extreme sports. For some, sport is second nature – the aim is to play it though, not just watch it! There are several important reasons to take exercise.

- It makes your body work more efficiently; you sleep more readily and more soundly, have improved circulation, better posture and overall strength and endurance.

- Physical activity releases serotonin, the neurotransmitter which makes you feel good.

- You can't be doing anything else when you are taking physical exercise; this frees up the mind and broadens your capacity to generate creativity and do some problem solving.

Alcohol and other substances   You were recently a student yourself and maybe you got smashed regularly. Perhaps you still want to. This is up to you, but if you get legless during the working week you will not be able to function at an optimum level in the classroom. Unless you are one of the fortunate few who never gets hangovers it's just not worth it. If you drink late into the night the alcohol will be in your bloodstream the next morning and this puts your self-control at risk. It is also likely to still be on your breath – bad idea.

Deciding whether or not to go sick

Most teachers are conscientious to a fault. They know their absence has a significant impact on students and possibly on colleagues so drag themselves into school regardless. Sometimes this is counter-productive. They take longer to fully recover and under perform in the meantime; they are also generous with spreading their germs. As a rule of thumb don't go into work if you have a temperature more than one degree over the norm or are spending serious time in the bathroom. If you are taking painkillers every few hours you will be unable concentrate on teaching: you are also likely to be short tempered and not react to difficulties well. If you think you could stay at home and perhaps read a book or watch daytime TV you are probably not ill enough to take a sick day. If in any doubt go into school and see how it goes. If you go downhill during the day you know it is serious enough to stay home tomorrow. It is not uncommon for teachers to work flat out all term and get ill on the very last day as they begin to relax. If this might be you, have a few days at home before you go away on holiday. This will ensure that your time of relaxation is used to best effect.

TIME RESOURCES

Lack of time is a constant complaint in education. Having more demands than time available is one of the greatest stresses for teachers. In a survey in the UK, workload was given as the main reason for teachers leaving the profession, considerably more significant than dealing with student behaviour (Smithers and Robinson, 2003). Workload threatens motivation when there isn't time to do things properly and priorities appear to be dictated by bureaucratic processes rather than the perceived needs of the students. Inevitably much of the time that needs to be organized is outside the school day. Spending Sunday evenings head down getting ready for the week rather than having a night out with mates is a common scenario for teachers.

New teachers are especially vulnerable to time pressures as everything is new. Not only do you have to find out all about your school and the students you also have to find time to prepare your first lessons. Things do get better as you become more experienced and develop a bank of knowledge, skills and resources to draw on.

It sounds obvious but not everyone realizes that time is a finite resource: it does not expand or increase. People respond in several ways to time issues and if you are honest with yourself you will know which of the following is true for you.

Reacting to demands as they arise

This can work temporarily but is not helpful in the longer term. It means you are constantly dictated to by the urgent rather than finding time for the important. You eventually come to a point when several things need doing at once or you are unable to respond effectively to what needs attention right now. The result is fragmentation, leaving things half finished and a feeling of panic as your ability to keep up starts to slip.

Working all the time

This is a common scenario for teachers who see little alternative if they are to keep their heads above the flood of demands. The risk is burn-out, physical or mental illness and possibly damaged relationships. It is both unreasonable and unrealistic to do this. Work out what your limits are and question the wisdom of taking on anything that goes beyond them.

Thinking that you are working all the time!

Sometimes the reality is that you constantly procrastinate. You respond at length to unplanned interruptions and get easily distracted; you have no idea 'where the time goes' but the work is still there to be done. If this seems true for you keep a diary to identify how much you might be able to recoup from the time you waste. Simple strategies like finishing one task before starting another, leaving the phone to take messages or giving yourself a time limit on open-ended tasks might ease your stress overnight.

Planning time

You can do this by being rigid or being flexible. A rigid framework leaves no room for the unexpected or for moving priorities around. This is all very well until unexpected demands inevitably appear. A flexible framework is about being realistic and takes account of your own organizational style and needs and the actual demands of the situation in which you are working. A simple example is to not attempt 'thinking and planning' activities where and when you are likely to be constantly interrupted. Identify your own patterns for mental acuity. Some individuals are at their best early in the morning, others later in the day.

It can help to plan on a weekly and termly basis. If you know when there will be higher demands you can organize yourself in advance so these times are not more stressful than they need be. Spending fifteen minutes sorting your diary into priorities at the beginning of the week can save time later on. There is evidence that carefully planning your first day in school to take account of relationship building, establishing expectations and clarifying procedures is related to positive outcomes for the next eight weeks – an excellent use of time (Worsham and Emmer, 1983).

Here are ideas that may help with time management in your first year or two of teaching. The earlier you can get to grips with these the better.

Preparing lessons Be clear about curriculum expectations for the whole term. Ask about materials that already exist and how to access these. Decide which you will use, amend or replace. If you are still in training or in touch with fellow students who teach the same subject discuss sharing ideas and materials. Use the Internet for ideas to support your teaching – it's an amazing resource.

Find out about audiovisual aids so you have access to a wide range of different presentation resources, some of which you will not have to prepare yourself. Check arrangements for setting up any IT equipment you may want to use.

Work in collaboration with students. Plan small groups to present findings of their research on topics from time to time. This boosts self-esteem, self-efficacy and learning outcomes.

Don't re-invent the wheel next year. Organize your curriculum resources so you can access them quickly in the future. Plan a pack of flexible lessons to use in an emergency. These can be games, structured discussions or other activities adaptable to a wide range of curriculum needs.

Administration Keep reports brief. Bear in mind your audience and what they need to know. Parents will devote time to reading (and re-reading) what you have written. Do not waste time or energy in negativity; ensure comments are constructive.

Plan time for basic organization such as filing. This avoids spending valuable time trying to find what you 'are sure you put down here somewhere' and you don't end up in a panic doing things at the last minute.

General BANJO stands for Bang A Nasty Job Off (Black, 1987). Sometimes we waste time and energy putting something off because it is annoying or not straightforward. When we finally get down to it, it may be less effort than we anticipated. Save yourself the additional stress.

You do not have to do everything to high distinction standard. You will burn yourself out in no time. Look at what is important to do well and where it makes less difference if you cut corners. Some things might not be necessary at all. Think why you are doing something and judge your input by the outcomes.

Be wary of taking on too much too soon. Give yourself time to settle into the job before you pick up options to volunteer. Enthusiasm is a gift to the profession but use it wisely. Some people take on extra work because they believe they need to prove themselves. You would do better in your first year to concentrate on developing confidence in carrying out the essential tasks.

Look at where you can double up tasks: for example, if you have a long journey to school think of ways you might constructively use this time in thinking and planning.

Delegate: some tasks can be delegated; students may enjoy taking on a responsibility or helping you out. It won't help you or them, however, if you get them to stay in and do things for you as a punishment.

Time for behaviour management

The students who cause you the most difficulties are often the most needy and demanding of your time and attention. This additional time is usually not planned for and has to come from nowhere. This then impacts on your stress at several levels. Your response may therefore be sharper and more irritable than it might otherwise be.

You may believe you have no time to promote positive behaviour, teach expectations, foster good relationships or run individual interventions for students. Some people take the view that they should not have to do this as part of their teaching. They then have to find time to react to repeated incidents of unwanted behaviour. Planning brings the control of situations back to you and within the boundaries of your own time management. Being pro-active about behaviour management does not mean you never have a crisis but it certainly reduces their frequency. You will find more on this in Chapters 4 and 7.

Making time for relaxation

What do you like doing which has nothing whatsoever to do with your job? Whether it is sport, socializing, painting or just reading the paper, make time for it! You can get so buried in your head by the job that you lose perspective. If you don't make time for your family and friends, you will also alienate your best sources of support in time of need. If it seems you never have time for your partner put it in your planning schedule.

EMOTIONAL RESOURCES

It is crucial that you maintain your emotional resilience. This will make all the difference to your survival in the classroom. A high level of positive emotional energy helps you to stay calm in a crisis, extends your ability to be patient, enables you to remain with the possible and positive and pick yourself up after a bad day. Low emotional energy leads to ill considered reactions, and means you will more easily be deflated, defeated and overwhelmed. You need to get and stay on the upward spiral.

How you feel is not only related to what happens to you but also how you think about yourself in the job. You probably have more choices than you realize. Maximizing emotional resources also means identifying where your support lies and how and when to access this.

What depletes emotional energy?

- Feeling undervalued.
- Feeling blamed or ridiculed.
- Feeling you are not in control of situations.
- Fearing you are ineffective.
- Feeling ambivalent about what you are doing.
- Being worn down by efforts that appear to have no positive outcome.
- Feeling overwhelmed and exhausted by constant demands, not being able to prioritize.
- Trying to be all things to all people.
- Other people's distress.
- Feeling guilty.
- Feeling scrutinized.
- Feeling isolated.

CONTINUED

- Tedium.
- Poor communications – not knowing what is going on leads to anxiety.
- Keeping up appearances all the time.
- Negativity.

What enhances emotional energy?

- Having evidence that you and your efforts are valued.
- Seeing that you are making a difference – getting some positive feedback.
- Having positive relationships.
- Constructive conversations.
- Feeling you are aware of what is going on.
- Feeling you can influence events.
- Believing what you are doing is worthwhile.
- Having some control over what happens to you.
- Feeling you belong.
- Variety.
- Experiencing laughter – it relieves tension.
- Experiencing warmth – it is comforting and reassuring.
- Feeling life is balanced – keeping a 'big picture' perspective.
- Being able to be yourself.

There are ways you can maximize your emotional resources, regardless of the challenges you face. Some are dependent on other people and some you can put in place yourself. If you are fortunate to be working in an emotionally literate school where everyone is aware of these issues you will have a much higher level of emotional resources than if you work somewhere where the only feelings that rise regularly to the surface are the negative ones.

Emotional support from others

Your relationships with others can help maintain your emotional resources in several different ways. The following are not necessarily the same individuals.

- People who 'take you out of yourself'. These are the friends who encourage you to have a good time and help you relax.

- People who value you, boost your self-esteem and think you are just great. If you are one of the lucky ones these will be members of your family as well as your long-time supporters. Children can also be an excellent source of uncritical positive feedback.

- Colleagues who acknowledge how hard you are working and are helpful and constructive rather than critical when things don't go so well.

- Confidantes – those with whom you share your inner feelings. Discuss your concerns with trusted people but be careful to maintain reciprocity in the relationship. If you are really distressed and need to talk over and over the same issues then the relationship may stop being an equal one. Go and see a professional counsellor.

Cherish all the relationships in your life that boost your sense of self – whether they are with family, friends or colleagues. These are the ones that you pay attention to.

Be an emotional support to yourself

Nearly all of us have a critical inner voice that from time to time either tells us we are rubbish or tells us that other people are a waste of space. Neither of these messages is useful, either personally or professionally. They make us feel bad about ourselves or about other people. We need to take control of these voices and not let them run amok with our feelings. Counteracting the negative voices requires some determination but can be done. Try the following.

- When an incident leaves you feeling useless, focus on what you have learnt for next time.

- Remind yourself it is OK to make mistakes and that everyone does it. Biographies about famous people invariably include down times as well as successful ones.

- Focus on achievements, however small – for yourself and your students.

- Get a positive feedback file; put in it anything that is said or given to you that makes you feel good, such as cards, comments, letters. Include all the little notes and positives you get from your students. Take it out when you are feeling unvalued (as we all do from time to time) and remember that you are not.

- Have conversations with positive people – avoid the whingers and the doom merchants.

- When you feel so overwhelmed with strong feelings that you can't think straight, give yourself permission to not make decisions on the spot. You can almost always come back to them later.

- Be aware that there are choices in how you see and interpret the world and therefore choices in how you feel.

- Have loud conversations with your inner voices in the privacy of your car – it puts them in their place and may give you (and perhaps a few other drivers) some unexpected moments of amusement!

- Don't jump to conclusions or make assumptions too quickly. Our fears and imaginings about other people's motivations and purposes are often worse than reality. Check things out before you waste too much of your precious emotional resources.

- Work out what comforts and de-stresses you. It is different for everyone. What has worked for you in the past?

- Use music to change your mood. Whether its rock, Beethoven or baroque, an immersion in sound can take you out of yourself more quickly than anything.

- Have fun. Give yourself permission to have regular spaces to do whatever raises your spirits. Don't even think about work during this time – it is your gift to be treasured.

Jenny Mosley, who has written widely on circle time, talks about the usefulness of linking hard times and serious challenges with serious rewards. She cites the example of choosing a supportive inner voice when confronted with the most difficult student in the class. 'Come on, do your worst, one more insult and I get an aromatherapy massage!' (Mosley, 1993).

When you feel at your most despondent, angry or confused, stay with and reflect on the feeling for a while because it helps you understand your most difficult and damaged students. Bear in mind that you probably have more support to help deal with things than they do.

Getting things into perspective

I was once hitch hiking in Spain and was by the roadside in Zaragoza for hours and hours, failing to get a lift. I was getting into a state of despair, anxiety and frustration when suddenly this single question popped into my head: 'When you look back on this day in six months time how much will it matter?' The answer of course was not a lot. I was using up a great deal of emotional energy for little impact. I decided to calm down and enjoy the view. Within a little while a car stopped and took me all the way home to London. Ever since I have asked myself the same question in trying times, 'Is this a Zaragoza moment or not?' It helps to get things in perspective.

SUMMARY

The message of this chapter is simple. Look after yourself well and maximize all the resources that are in your control. This will enable you to function at the optimum level in your work. If you do this you have more chance of being effective with all students but especially those who are more demanding of you.

Chapter 4

You and Your Class

This chapter is about establishing the relationships you want to have with all your students. The ideas and approaches here help prevent difficult situations from arising in the first place. They maximize the chances of everyone having a good time.

In your teacher role you are in a position of authority. How you demonstrate that authority is important. This chapter encourages you to think through the various positions you might take with your class group and their potential outcomes. It shows you how to stay in charge of proceedings but also develop respectful interactions that provide for some choice and enhance self-control.

Many studies outline the qualities of an effective teacher. These include skills, personal characteristics and classroom climate (Hay McBer, 2000). Characteristics include being infectiously optimistic, a good listener, showing commitment, a taker of blame and a celebrator of others and having a clear philosophy (Brighouse, 2000, cited in Sharp, 2001). This chapter outlines how to develop approaches and skills that produce an optimal classroom climate.

THINK POSITIVE

The vast majority of students are OK. They may be noisy, lively, cheeky and a bit challenging but with the right approach you will get along together and they will not make your life a misery. Take the 'wrong' approach and you will be digging a hole for yourself. There is every reason to believe that unhelpful or unskilled responses from teachers exacerbate and entrench some difficulties that would otherwise evaporate. The emphasis here is on what is meant by 'the right approach'.

There will be a few students having a rough time because of what is currently happening in their lives. Difficult students are usually dealing with difficult circumstances and school needs to be a safe place. Although you and your biggest challenges are the focus of Chapter 7, read this chapter first. Good practice for all students is good practice for challenging students and vice versa. Your response to students who are hard to manage will impact on the rest of your class.

Your primary approach to all students need not, however, be determined by the potential impact of a few. Your days do not have to be prescribed by fear of what might happen if you don't keep a tight rein. You have a choice. Either you go into the fray prepared 'to get the better of them' or you think about how to encourage self-discipline in your students within an atmosphere of positive relationships and mutual respect.

You can see the classroom as a battleground, where the strongest win and the toughest survive. Plenty of teachers embark on the next round every time they go through the door. Others have given up and believe the students already have the upper hand. Their aim is just to get through the lesson, somehow, anyhow. They make little effort to make the lesson lively and interesting – 'what's the point?' The battlers, the bereft and the cynics in the staffroom agree – it's hell out there.

But many teachers do not believe this is the case, and have chosen to view their interactions in the classroom differently. There are certainly issues of power and control in the classroom, but there are several ways of thinking about this. It is wise to take action on the basis of considered alternatives. This chapter provides you with information on which to weigh up your options: it shows which factors facilitate a positive outcome and which make it more difficult.

Expectations

One of the difficulties for new teachers is to be clear about what behaviour they require in the classroom.

- Is it important that students are quiet and listen? Always? If not, in what circumstances?

- Should everyone do as they are asked immediately?

- When does a question become an argument? What does this mean?

- Is bad language OK so long as it isn't intentionally abusive or do you make a point of pulling students up on every four letter word you hear?

- Should students be allowed to eat in class?

- When is helping each other cheating?

You can find answers to some of these questions by checking behaviour policies (see Chapter 5: You and Your School). If specifics are not included then find out what other teachers do. You need to work as far as possible within the culture of the school and most of that will not be written down. What is acceptable in an inner city high school is unlikely to be the same as in a primary school in a wealthy suburb. You cannot address everything. Some things are important for the effective running of your class and some are best ignored.

Small children come into school with a range of different experiences and expectations. Some have routines and values that mirror those of the school, others do not. It is important to teach children what is expected and give them opportunities to practice and be rewarded for compliance. Too many pupils in their first school get labelled as having 'behaviour problems' before they have had a chance to discover some good feelings about other ways of being (Roffey and O'Reirdan, 2001). Teenagers, too, benefit from some basic instruction on expectations. High school teachers who spend time with students practising coming into the classroom in an orderly way are more likely to have settled classes sooner and save time in the long run.

Expectations are more than complying with specific routines. If you expect your students to be just wonderful this can be a self-fulfilling prophecy – if you expect them to be the worst in the school they will live up to the reputation and expectation.

One year six class was encouraged to think of themselves as the best in the school and that they had been allocated their particular teacher because of this. The students will tell you that they were hand picked. The results they are achieving compared to the previous year are amazing. The truth is that, for several reasons, they were a class that was failing. The change is in their expectations of themselves and what they felt their teacher required of them.

Focus on what is going well and reinforce the behaviour you want

Acknowledgement is highly rewarding. Give attention to what you want, not to what you don't want. Comment positively on students who are doing as you have requested. Avoid a simple 'well done' but state 'well done for . . .'. Thank or acknowledge conforming students before you comment on non-compliance, especially those near students having more difficulty. This is known as 'proximity praise' and works a treat (Canter and Canter, 1976).

If students are still not conforming remind them before reprimanding them. 'What have I asked you to do?' is less confrontational than 'Why aren't you doing what I told you?' Asking questions that gain a definite 'yes' response lead to a more cooperative class. For example, 'Is everyone clear about the instructions?'; 'Has everyone got a pencil?'

Almost everyone responds well to positive feedback but be careful how you do it. Some children just don't respond well to praise. Comments should be brief, genuine and specific. Just a thumbs up can be useful sometimes. Second hand praise is especially effective. Tell a parent, other teacher or anyone (!) about a student's achievements either in their hearing or where you know the positive messages will get back to them.

Another way to focus on the positive is to occasionally give out raffle tickets for specific behaviours – such as excellent clearing up, kindness to others. In a primary class the raffle can be called on Friday afternoon and five students could get small prizes, such as chocolates or special pencils. In a secondary school class, the raffle could be held every half term and the prizes fewer but worth more – perhaps a voucher for a local café. It is important that the children who have most difficulty complying get sufficient rewards to motivate them.

Some teachers find whole class reinforcement even more useful. The 'marbles in the jar' strategy means dropping a marble or button into a jar every time a specific behaviour is noted from an individual or group. The whole class gets a treat when the jar is full. The teacher monitors how quickly the jar gets filled. This has to be soon enough to maintain interest but not too easily achieved either. Marbles do not get taken out for any reason (Canter and Canter, 1976).

Rules, regulations, rewards and sanctions

Spend time with students at the beginning of the year working out the ground rules for interaction in the classroom. What do they think is reasonable? Ensure that everyone gets a say, so that decisions are not dominated by a few loud voices.

Encourage rules beginning with 'do' rather than 'don't' and keep the list brief. Spend time talking about what these mean in practice and defining words such as 'respect'.

Students do need to know there are consequences for continuous unacceptable behaviour. It should be clear what these are. It is important to grade rewards but even more important to grade sanctions and consequences. Research shows that it is the consistency of sanctions that is effective, not the severity. Strong punishment for a minor misdemeanour leaves nothing in reserve for serious incidents (Comerford and Jacobson, 1987). Always give choices to comply and warnings before consequences are imposed.

Though you may never need it, having a safety net of agreed school strategies for extreme behaviour can be reassuring, You will know what to do if and when necessary.

Testing you out

Be prepared! Nearly all student groups test out new teachers to find out how they respond. This is not necessarily all the students in a class, but some take on that role while the rest watch with great interest. Expect to be challenged, cheeked and checked! Shock, horror and defensiveness are rarely helpful responses. You need to keep your cool and composure. You will establish credibility if you respond with lightness and humour while making it very clear what you consider acceptable or not. This enables you to stay in control of yourself and the situation. Becoming angry, defensive or embarrassed indicates that you have, to some extent, lost it.

LINKS BETWEEN PARENTING AND PEDAGOGIC STYLES

Within the school environment teachers are 'in loco parentis'. They are supposed to take the place of parents in caring for students responsibly.

There has been much research carried out on various parenting styles and their outcomes (Baumrind, 1971, 1991; Steinberg et al, 1994) and it is worth making connections with teaching styles. Note that these are described here in stereotypical forms. Most parents and teachers have elements of these styles. The first two described here are more likely to surface under stress (see Chapter 3: You and Your Resources for reducing stress levels).

Permissive parenting

This style is warm and responsive but does not set any clear expectations or boundaries. Children are not unloved but are all over the place. Basically they are allowed to do much as they like and demand what they want. Parents may be human doormats: walked all over by tyrannical toddlers or jumping at their older child's beck and call. There is little tuning into the process of parenting, which means that expectations do not change with age and development. No one helps children to make good decisions or to problem-solve effectively. There is poor consistency and consequently not much sense of security. There is little expectation that others have to be taken into consideration or that waiting for something is perfectly acceptable. This parenting style may have its roots in a philosophy of child-centred development and the importance of freedom of expression. More often it comes about because parents don't know what else to do or are too stressed and exhausted to stand their ground or follow anything through.

The permissive teacher: the child-sitter role Such teachers are likely to say that the kids are just great – to start out with at least. Being liked by the students is often important to them so they don't make any demands that might rock the boat. In these classrooms 'anything goes'. Teachers may be friendly and responsive but are not very pro-active or organized. Things happen haphazardly and before long students may turn the classroom into an indoor playground. Students might like this at some level but it does not raise their self-esteem and eventually their behaviour simply deteriorates. Learning takes place incidentally rather than in structured ways. School students might like such teachers but do not respect them. Even good students become demotivated by classroom chaos.

CASE STUDY

Andy was getting on for 40 but he did his best to wear what the high school students were wearing, including a couple of piercings. He patted the boys on the back and called them 'mate' and talked football and horse racing to a select few who shared his passions. He rarely took much time to prepare for lessons so the exercises he did give were

CONTINUED

simply copied from texts. He got round to marking these eventually. Some of the more committed students got through his lessons this way and achieved exam passes. He managed the more difficult students by letting them talk about music or films or sport. They didn't do well. Andy thought he was a great teacher.

Some teachers end up being permissive by default. They have tried to assert control and it hasn't worked. These teachers are often those who were not very confident to start with and quickly lose the will to establish order.

Outcomes   If age-appropriate demands are not made on children they have nothing to respond to. If other people do things for them all the time they do not learn to stick at anything or become independent. This leads to immaturity, over-dependence and impulsive behaviour. The research indicates that negative outcomes are particularly evident for boys who do not achieve well (Baumrind, 1971). Children need structure and consistency if they are to become independent learners. The permissive teacher is not doing the students any favours. Pupils are likely to recognize this and lose their respect.

Authoritarian parenting

This is where we see high control but also low warmth. In an authoritarian family children are expected to do as they are told – or else. It is the 'do as I say, not as I do' school of parenting. There is a high value on conformity and obedience and little value placed on negotiation or flexibility. Adults are supposed to be respected just because they are adults. Authoritarian parents do not take into account that children have different needs at different ages. It is not surprising that they resort to punishment most often.

The authoritarian teacher: the police officer role   You can sometimes hear authoritarian teachers as you walk around a school. They are the ones who are shouting and laying down the law. Rules are not agreed or negotiated but imposed. Whatever the volume of their voices you do not see these teachers do much listening. They do not ask, they tell.

Such individuals are primarily concerned about maintaining control within the school organization; they are not interested in developing relationships. Consequently they are not likely to see strengths as well as deficits in individuals. It is easier for an authoritarian teacher to label and blame rather than accept the ambiguity of a whole person. They can be bullies to both students and other staff alike. Authoritarian teachers who mirror authoritarian parents will frighten smaller children and may be on a collision course with adolescents. Many teenagers are intent on rebelling against authority of any sort – you may be headed for some time consuming challenges if this is your chosen approach.

CASE STUDY

Mustapha, aged 14, was frequently absent from school. His mother could not speak English and often kept him home to translate for her when she went to the doctor's or to the housing office. The family were struggling to afford proper school uniform and this was another reason for his absences. One of the senior teachers suggested that Mustapha came to school in his ordinary clothes until the issue of uniform could be sorted out. The next day Mustapha came into school late to be met by another of the senior management team. Without giving the boy a

CONTINUED

chance to explain he shouted that the school rules were not to be flouted and Mustapha was not going to be allowed into school without the appropriate clothing. Mustapha swore at him and did not come to school again for a term.

Outcomes   Younger children may be anxious, even fearful of authoritarian approaches. They are often withdrawn and certainly unhappy. As they get older they become more and more angry. Sadly they relate to others in a hostile way and may be isolated from their peers. There is a potential gender difference where girls lack the willingness to explore the world and boys show high levels of defiance. Children who live in families where there is violence show similar outcomes. The boys' anger and defiance, however, often masks a high level of depression and anxiety (Sternberg et al, 1993; Jaffe et al, 1986).

Students may behave well out of fear when an authoritarian teacher is present but when they are not there the students run wild. Bullying behaviour is modelled as permissible. Pupils who are always told what to do are denied the opportunity to learn self-control and decision-making. They develop an 'external locus of control' which means they do not take responsibility for their own actions.

Authoritative/facilitative parenting

Authoritative parents make reasonable, age-appropriate demands on their children but are also warm and responsive to their needs. Relationships and communication are valued highly. Authoritative parents have clear expectations and values and are consistent about boundaries. Children know where they stand. However these boundaries are not fixed in stone for all time and are flexible and negotiated according to age and level of responsibility. Children are encouraged to be involved in decision-making. Facilitative parents give their children the skills to become independent. Rather than being controlling they encourage the development of self-control. They model appropriate social behaviours and provide a foundation for problem solving and other life skills. Authoritative families pay great attention to the process of parenting rather than goals. Children are encouraged to

be the best that they can be, not what parents have pre-determined they should be.

The authoritative/facilitative teacher: the conductor role Such teachers have high expectations of students but are also sensitive to classroom dynamics and to individual needs. They are able to be flexible in delivering the curriculum. Students are guided and encouraged, not dictated to. This enables students to develop self-control in the classroom rather than having control imposed. Teachers who are like conductors are very aware of what is going on. They pick up on potentially difficult interactions and take quick action to prevent escalation.

In a five-year study looking at differences between effective and ineffective teachers, Kounin identified that it was the way that teachers pre-empted troublesome behaviour that made the difference (Kounin, 1971). He summarized these teacher skills as 'withitness', 'overlapping', 'momentum' and 'smoothness'. All of these indicate high awareness of what is going on in the classroom and of being in charge of procedures. Such a teacher

- has well established routines for students – for example, how to gain attention, enter a class

- is well prepared and has clear expectations for the lesson

- gives clear instructions to the class group while moving towards students who are beginning to disrupt

- gives attention to individuals and small groups without having his back to the rest of the class

- scans the class frequently

- has brief interactions with many students rather than lengthy ones with a few

- changes the direction and pace of a lesson if students are becoming restless

- prepares students for transitions between activities – gives notice that they are coming to the end of one activity and concise instructions about the next task

- lets students know by presence, eye contact or gesture that she is aware of any unwanted behaviour

- pays minimal attention to minor disruptions so as not to disrupt the flow of the lesson

- informs students regularly how they are doing

- gives positive feedback

- keeps all students involved and active

- encourages 'accountability' or demonstrations of engagement such as asking questions.

Kounin also coined a term he called 'the Ripple Effect'. This refers to how a teacher's way of handling unwanted behaviour affects others in the class. Giving a rationale for behaviour works well, such as 'Silence while I give instructions means no-one loses out'. Firmness and a concerned emotional engagement rather than blandness in interactions both have a positive ripple effect. Showing anger or irritability does not promote wanted behaviour from other students.

Outcomes   Children who grow up with authoritative parenting have the best outcomes. Because they are expected to think for themselves and make decisions they develop a sense of self-efficacy and self-confidence. Authoritative teachers bring the students along with them and provide them with the skills to learn self-discipline. Some students are not used to this and at the outset may run wild when they see someone not behaving as a disciplinarian. Clear, consistent negotiated boundaries are the way to begin.

BEING A FACILITATIVE TEACHER

The following shows some of the different ways a facilitative teacher might operate.

A purposeful classroom

Arrive at your class punctually – it gives messages about your own organization and also about caring for the students. They matter enough for you to be there on time.

Establish ways of entering the classroom and getting settled. Everyone pushing and shoving does not set up a helpful ambience. Ask students to give you a certain signal when they are ready to start, perhaps just seated and looking your way.

There are hundreds of interactions a day between pupils and teachers and you can't pay equal attention to all of them – it's exhausting. It is valuable to spend a little time establishing regular routines in your classroom. This means making sure that expectations are clear, consistent and predictable so everyone knows what to do and how to do it. This contributes to an atmosphere of stability, reassurance and success. Phrase expectations positively and display a short list, no more than seven, at eye level centrally in the class.

Your students will be more engaged with learning if you are well prepared. This includes.

- curriculum content: what you intend to cover

- relevance and meaning: ways of tuning into student interest

- differentiation: providing for the different learning needs in your class

- materials and equipment: having all you need in working order.

You need to know what your lessons will be covering in terms of the curriculum and how you are going to incorporate your students' lives so that they can relate to the material. There is good evidence to show that making content meaningful in some way to students and building on their knowledge, however unconnected this may seem to be, initiates engagement with the curriculum and this in turn limits behavioural difficulties (Assor, Kaplan and Roth, 2002).

Do not begin the lesson until you have the attention of your students. This does not necessarily mean everyone should be completely silent and looking your way but nearly all are fairly quiet and looking expectant. If you have students who have a struggle settling down engage them actively as soon as possible – perhaps to give out materials.

Be clear about what you expect.

- Give students the 'Big Picture' at the beginning of the lesson. This is what the learning aims are, what you will be covering and what you hope they will be achieving. If your lesson is properly prepared you will be able to do this easily.

- Do not give too much information at once about what to do – especially for anyone who learns more slowly. No-one can manage more than seven pieces of information at a time and most of us are more comfortable with much less.

- Give information in both verbal and visual modes (Smith, 1998).

- Ensure that everyone can participate in a way that ensures they have some success as well as challenges.

● Students are most likely to comply with requests that are clear, direct and courteous (Kellerman and Shea, 1996).

Remember the following ancient Chinese saying – it still holds true.

● We hear and we forget.

● We see and we remember.

● We do and we understand.

Communicate procedures about what should happen when students are unsure what to do – for example, 'Check what you have been told or is written down, ask the person sitting next to you, and put your hand up to indicate you need help if you still don't know'.

Let students know what they are expected to do when they have completed work:

● Choice of activity – which activities can they choose from?

● Extension work?

● Help others?

● A democratic classroom

This classroom fosters fairness, an equal say and responsibility within the group. Do your best to treat everyone equally. There are bound to be students you warm to more than others but it is unwise to show you have favourites. 'Teacher's pet' is not comfortable either for the favoured student or the others. This also applies to challenging students with whom you are trying to develop positive relationships (see Chapter 7). Similarly, do not jump to conclusions about who might be a culprit in an escapade. Pupils will complain unfairly that they are being picked on but on occasions this really is the case. Be as even-handed as possible.

Making things equitable and fair means making sure everyone gets their turn. For special responsibilities and privileges make a chart so that individuals can see when it will be theirs. Do not withdraw routine privileges as a sanction.

Invite and encourage everyone to participate. Foster self-reflection and self-evaluation so that students do not become overly dependent on praise received for 'pleasing the teacher'. Make positive feedback specific (Larrivee, 2002).

Ensure students have opportunities to make choices where possible; even simple things like the order in which assignments are done can give students a sense of control in an otherwise teacher controlled environment.

Questions fuel thinking – do not always have the answers, let the students show you that they know things you don't sometimes. Acknowledge their superior knowledge!

Walk the talk

- Behave at all times in ways you want the students to: you then have every right to say, 'It is unacceptable for you to speak to me like that, I do not speak to you that way'.

- Model negotiation and compromise.

- Be prepared to say you are sorry if you think you did not handle something well.

Do not demand that students say sorry to each other – it is usually meaningless. Most pupils have a very acute sense of fairness, especially in middle childhood. Ask them to come up with a suggestion to show how they are going to even things up. Doing sorry is better than saying sorry.

Many students come into school expecting to be told what to do all the time. Changing the culture of the classroom is not an easy task. It may take time but do not believe the cynics who tell you that students are not capable of making good decisions for themselves. It is likely to be only true of those who have never had the chance.

A caring and inclusive classroom

Although teachers often say they are caring, pupils do not always appreciate this (Grote, 1995). It needs to be demonstrated in practice. If you convey to students that you value them you will be off to a good start. This includes certain expectations of work and behaviour – which you will help them meet. Listening to students is also central.

One obvious way to show students respect is simply to listen; listen to their complaints, listen to their triumphs and listen to their fears. It is amazing how many beginning teachers are so concerned with 'teaching', disseminating information and with lesson plans that they forget that a roomful of children wants to interact with them and to be listened to. In many classrooms, most students are never heard from. Their emotions and ideas are bottled up. Students in these environments think we just don't care about them, or we just don't want to hear what they have to say.

(Lockwood, 1995)

Start lessons by asking students a question. This gives the message that you are initiating a dialogue, not a monologue and that their contributions are both expected and welcome.

There is more on listening in Chapter 7.

Caring also means helping. Students who are unclear what to do need to know how to access guidance. Be clear about your procedures with this (see 'A purposeful classroom', above).

However exasperating they may be, telling students to 'shut-up' is demeaning and may fuel unnecessary rage. Also avoid saying work is 'easy' if they find it difficult – they may assume you think they are 'stupid'.

Personal bests It is hard for those individuals who are never a 'winner' to feel included. Competition need not always be between students. A system of 'personal bests' means that a student competes against himself. Can he do better than last time? This reduces the fear of failing compared to peers. Keeping a personal diary of 'personal best' achievements boosts self-esteem and self-efficacy. Individual achievement can continue to be celebrated for everyone.

Statements which incorporate care for an aggressor as well as care for the aggrieved promotes an ethos of empathy: 'You are not allowed to hurt another student, other students are not allowed to hurt you'.

CASE STUDY

One college student, now training to be a teacher herself, commented on how she owed her future to one teacher. She was having difficulties at home and beginning to feel that school was a waste of time. This teacher showed belief in her and said he was not going to let her waste her ability. 'He cared about me, he made me work harder, made me feel that it mattered to him. I wouldn't be here at university if it wasn't for him'.

A caring classroom is also a safe and friendly one. This means that friendliness needs to be actively developed and any bullying behaviour immediately addressed (Roffey, Tarrant and Majors, 1994).

Differentiation Volumes have been written about differentiating the curriculum for an inclusive classroom. All students need to have appropriate learning expectations and experience success. The downside of differentiation is that it can take up considerable time in planning. Get into a routine pattern so that it becomes easier for you and expectations for your students are clear.

A peaceful classroom

Avoid conflict by having enough of the right equipment or a clear rota for use of scarce materials.

Allow time for activities to begin and end. Give pupils with the most difficulty warning of transitions.

Some students, particularly younger children, will react more to the sound of your voice than to the words that are said. Shouting raises the emotional level. Some teachers manage to get attention without shouting. Here are some of the ways they do this.

Younger students

- When you first enter a class make it clear what you will do to gain attention. Ask the students if they have any ideas.

- Ask students to pass messages to the others that you are ready to speak.

- Give signals that each person then copies until everyone is waiting quietly. Raise your hand and everyone raises theirs and looks at you – hands on head or fingers on noses, everyone should do the same thing!

- Clap in a rhythm and ask the students to copy.

- Patting your knees can work well too – everyone joins in.

- Proximity praise – comment to those who are waiting well.

High school students

- Say you will give students many opportunities to speak and contribute and that you will listen but you cannot talk to them while they are talking to each other.

- Negotiate how to do it.

- A hand in the air – a message around the class (see 'Younger students' above).

- Sports teachers often use whistles to good effect – you could also use a something similar but less piercing in the classroom – like a small bell or a light gavel on the desk. Alter what you use for fun sometimes – a tambourine or a hooter perhaps. Get students to bring something in.

- With very difficult classes it may be better to get students settled in groups.

- Give plenty of opportunity for discussion in the class.

Teach simple mediation skills to address minor conflicts between students. Many schools have trained peer mediators to help address less serious issues. This is the very basic outline – read about methods in more detail before you put this in place (Cornelius and Faire, 1989).

1   Both students need to agree to mediate.

2   Each has the opportunity to say how they see what happened, what they feel and what they would like to happen now.

3   Each student listens to the other.

4   They are asked to brainstorm solutions.

5   They agree on one to put into practice.

You can use quiet music to help re-establish a sense of calm, and relaxation activities may also be helpful at times.

A fun classroom

New teachers have an advantage over others who have been in the job much longer and may have become a bit stale and tired. Students respond well to enthusiasm. A teacher with energy and ideas has a better chance of engaging pupils than one who is jaded. Students respond less well to teachers who are so anxious they cannot think creatively or flexibly. Particularly in the primary classroom, teachers who are 'larger than life' may have the edge.

Humour can be a great way of generating a positive classroom atmosphere. It can enhance inter-personal relationships and a feeling of belonging. Everyone having a laugh at the same thing bonds people together: it also relieves stress. Ensure that no-one laughs at someone else's expense.

Teachers who are able to make fun of themselves from time to time, admit they don't know something and apologize for sometimes not getting things right are more likely to have positive interactions with students.

Classes in fun classrooms have pace and diversity. There are a variety of activities to reinforce the curriculum content. These include toys, tricks, magic, acting and games.

Paula Pane   A child is drawn on the window of the primary classroom. Addressing Paula Pane depersonalizes critical messages to the whole group – 'Oh Paula, what should I do, there are at least three children here who aren't taking any notice at all'. It can also be used to reinforce positive feedback – 'Hey, Paula, what do you think of this class, eh? Have you ever seen such good clearing up?' (Roffey and O'Reirdan, 2003).

The downside of the fun classroom is keeping a lid on excitement. Some students may see a fun activity as an opportunity to go wild. Pre-empt this by making your expectations very clear and giving a calming activity before the end of the lesson.

CIRCLE TIME PHILOSOPHY AND PRACTICE FOR DEMOCRACY, CARING, INCLUSION AND FUN

Known in different places as circle time, the magic circle, and sharing circles, this class activity provides a forum for promoting self-esteem, a positive class ethos, inclusion, peer support, emotional literacy and pro-social behaviours. It is most common in primary schools but has been successfully adapted for use in kindergarten and in high schools. Many teachers say it has turned their class around in giving students a greater sense of belonging and feeling good about being in school (Mosley, 1993; Weare, 2003). Other evaluations have shown that it enables students to reflect upon and regulate their behaviour (Robinson and Taylor, 1999), increases tolerance and develops empathy (Moss and Wilson, 1998). Behavioural difficulties decrease as a result (Doyle, 2003). Some teachers have circle time weekly, others more often. For small children 15 to 20 minutes is sufficient, 30–40 minutes for older students. It is important that circle time is not too long. Pupils appear to give circle time almost unqualified approval – they love doing it. Teachers are sometimes surprised by the impact on even the most difficult individuals.

The philosophy of the circle is crucial for its success. The teacher does not control the circle; he or she facilitates what happens. This approach enables students to feel safe and take responsibility for any problem-solving. Everyone sits in a circle to promote equality. No student is excluded unless they choose to be. No 'put-downs' are allowed, everyone gets a turn to speak while others listen, issues can be raised but individuals not named, everyone has an opportunity to pass. The class are given reminders of these rules at the beginning of every circle.

The following is a basic outline of how a primary class circle time session might look.

- Circle time begins with a simple greeting activity such as everyone introducing their neighbour or 'passing the smile'.

- Participants are then mixed up so that they sit next to different people. This happens several times during circle time. There are many ways of doing this such as everyone who is wearing green or all those who caught a bus to school change places.

- Students may then have a structured paired activity such as finding out what TV programs they both enjoy or how many brothers and sisters they have. Everyone takes turns to feed back findings to the whole group.

- Students all have a turn to complete sentences from simple stems, such as 'the best thing about this school is . . .'; to more personal ones: 'I feel happiest in school when . . .'; to problem solving ones: 'to stop bullying in this class we could . . .'

- Sometimes it is useful to have small groups brainstorm ideas and then feed back to the whole group. Ask for as many contributions as there are students in the group so everyone has a chance to speak.

- Self-esteem boosters are powerful. Some circles celebrate 'star of the day', where each individual gets a turn to receive positive accolades from their peers. As everyone gets their turn this creates an incentive to develop a class repertoire of positive statements.

- Once the class is skilled in the procedures and routines of circle time the circle can deal with issues that impinge on the class ethos, from bullying to borrowing.

- Sometimes it is easier for individuals to make statements about their experiences in 'silent statements', such as 'everyone who knows that bullying happens in this class change places'.

- It is helpful to close circle time with a calming activity such as a relaxation exercise or visualization.

If a pupil is 'silly' they are thanked for their contribution and then given the opportunity to say something else later. If a small group starts to be off task, a mix up activity can prevent this continuing.

If you think this is something that you would like to do in your class then ask for training or read one of the excellent books that are available before you start (see Chapter 8 for suggestions). It is a good idea for several teachers to embark on circle time together to support each other and share ideas. Circle time is at its most effective, however, when taken up by the whole school.

CASUAL STAFF

Some new teachers find themselves in casual employment after training and have to deal with new situations time and time again. There is little chance to build up the relationships which underpin good management. The following might help.

- Buy sticky labels and ask students to write their names on them so that you can at least address them by name. Do the same for yourself.

- Identify as quickly as possible who are the most influential students in the group and actively work with them to optimize the chance of peer pressure in your favour.

- Ask students about previous work and what they enjoyed about it. It shows interest and respect and you will clue into them as a group more quickly.

SUMMARY

This chapter has reminded you that as most students do not present you with challenging behaviour your class management should not be dictated by fear of the few. Pupils will, however, test you out to see what you are like and how much they can get away with. Your first task is to promote the behaviour you want.

We have explored various teaching styles in relation to maintaining order and demonstrated how optimum outcomes are linked to

CONTINUED

authoritative/facilitative styles. The most effective teachers remain in charge and aware of everything that is going on while offering choices, elements of control and respect to students. Such teachers are often able to intervene to stop disruptive behaviour before it takes hold. The chapter concluded with ideas to maximize student motivation and involvement in learning and to raise your own sense of efficacy and well-being in your teacher role.

Chapter 5

You and the School

The impact of school culture on new teachers is only just beginning to be fully recognized. School cultures are on the continuum from nurturing, positive and supportive, to cynical, negative and discouraging. Where an institution is placed on this continuum impacts not only on students but also on the adults who work there. As a consequence the emphasis is beginning to shift from strategies to cultures and the development of a collaborative ethos which addresses the emotional consequences for staff in dealing with challenging behaviour (Gamman, 2003). The way school staff talk about their work, and how they respond to new colleagues have a significant impact on how well the new recruit copes with the demands of their chosen profession (Bobek, 2002).

CASE STUDY

Angela is now in her third year of teaching and is in no doubt why she left her first school. 'It was a tough area, the kids were challenging but I was fine with that. In fact, the classroom was a haven compared to the staffroom . . . the bitchiness and bickering, the cliques. The way certain members of staff talked about some of the families was distressing. I was trying to put over a different point of view and the response was 'she'll learn'. A couple in particular raised their eyebrows at each other whenever I said anything. It was belittling. I ended up avoiding going in the staff room at all, just got on with things in the classroom at breaks and lunch time. I am now at another school and it is so different. People are friendly, positive. Staff talk about the kids like they really care about them, even when there is a problem. I can go and talk to the head teacher at any time and she is interested in what I have to say. I enjoy my work now, I don't have that knot in my stomach any more!'

THE DIFFERENCE A SCHOOL MAKES

You sense atmosphere when you walk into a school. You quickly pick up whether it is a happy or a stressful place to be. It is there on the faces of the students and of the staff, in the way they walk and talk, in how visitors are greeted and what is on the walls. If you get an interview try to visit in working time and see what you can pick up. These are things to look out for.

- Are most staff smiling or at least looking fairly relaxed or are they all rushing around with their eyebrows in a knot?

- What is the conversation in the staffroom like? Is it friendly chatter or are most people moaning about something?

- Do people say positive things about each other or do you hear mostly negativity and blame?

- Do adults speak warmly and positively to students or do you mostly hear shouted instructions usually beginning with the word 'don't'?

- Are students walking around in a fairly orderly way or is pushing and shoving the norm?

- Are walls used to display student work and positive images, or are they blank, dirty or defaced?

- Are you made to feel welcome by everyone you come into contact with or do people seem too busy to be bothered?

- Are students assigned to help you in any way and do they do that with pride and confidence?

If you get the chance ask students what they like most about their school. If they can't think of anything at all either get out of there – life is too short – or decide that making their lives more enjoyable is why you were born.

School X is a high school in a 'social priority' area near Sydney, Australia. There is a strong focus on individual and collective responsibility, led by the principal's example. This is illustrated by the whole school campaign on zero tolerance of graffiti. It had been a real problem that was tackled head on. Every class now has responsibility for an area of the school. Any graffiti is removed by the students in that class immediately regardless of who the perpetrator was. And – surprise, surprise – they don't have a problem any more. Both students and staff are developing a collective sense of pride in how their school looks. This adds to how much they feel valued. The principal smiles when he speaks of getting this initiative up and running – few said it would work.

STUDENTS WITH SPECIAL EDUCATIONAL NEEDS

Some schools accept all students whole-heartedly, assuming that, as a staff, they will be able to cope with a range of different needs. They focus on similarities to provide students with the closest possible educational experience to their peers. Others are dubious about anyone who does not fit the 'norm'. They focus primarily on differences and concerns about not having the necessary resources. Although relevant, inclusion is not only about resources but also a question of attitude, belief and confidence.

Many schools have on-site units or classes for students with behavioural needs. In reality these can either include or exclude children. The following is an illustration of positive thinking and good practice.

In this school's 'special class' a wide range of activities take place. These include reading and maths support, music and art, social and life skills, conflict resolution and cooperative games. The class is staffed by two specialist teachers with others timetabled for specific input as part of their workload. The specialist teachers work in the mainstream on occasions and also provide a consultation service for staff. Small groups

CONTINUED

of students are assigned to these special classes from the whole school. Some pupils spend a high proportion of their week in this class but pick up increasing amounts of time in mainstream as they learn how to manage difficult situations. Teachers are happy as they have some respite in their day and feel more supported. Keeping the classes open to everyone provides some good peer role models and reduces any stigma.

A SENSE OF BELONGING

Once you have secured a post you begin to think this is 'your' school. But belonging is not just your name on the staff list: it is also feeling that your presence matters and your contribution valued. Some teachers get this from the students alone and stay cocooned within their classroom. Others belong to a social or a departmental group. Hargreaves (1994) offers a model of healthy collaboration in which teachers have flexible alliances depending on the prevailing needs within a specific context. The focus is on continuous learning, improvement and active problem-solving. Many commentators speak favourably of the 'learning organization' (Stoll and Fink, 1995) where improvement is part of the culture, there is openness to new ideas and staff development is a priority. A large study of teachers in the United States who made effective adaptations to students had one thing in common: they all belonged to professional communities who 'encouraged and enabled them to transform their teaching' (McLaughlan and Talbert, 1993).

INDUCTION

Formal induction may take place over the first few weeks, but in reality you will be on a steep learning curve for most of your first year. Most schools will have an orientation process. Use this opportunity to the full while still a newcomer and do not be afraid to ask questions. You are entitled to clarification.

POLICIES, PROCEDURES AND PRACTICE

It is a great help if your school has a positive behaviour policy. If this has been drawn up in consultation with staff there is more likelihood of consistent application. If it has been drawn up in consultation with students even better. Such a policy needs to be a live document, regularly reviewed, monitored and communicated with the whole school community.

A positive management policy details what is expected of staff, students and others in promoting positive behaviour as well as responding to difficult and challenging behaviour. It should be clear about underlying principles for management and outline the rules, rewards and sanctions that are in operation.

Other policies are also worth reading in relation to behavioural issues – or at least knowing where to locate them in the school. Anti-bullying, equal opportunities/social justice, special needs and inclusion, attendance, child protection and any other welfare policy are all potentially helpful. If you don't have time to read them thoroughly just skim them and note anything important to know. It might be the school has taken on a specific discipline package in which case you need to enquire about training.

Whether or not anyone takes any notice of policies is another matter. In some schools there is congruence between the stated and the reality, in others there are wide discrepancies. A policy drawn up by one or two individuals is likely to gather dust on a shelf somewhere until someone needs to know what to do in an emergency. You need to check out how policies are put into operation. Observe what others do and ask questions about specifics. You are likely to find there are differences between members of staff. You then have the option of choosing an interpretation that is congruent with your approach. It is, however, unwise to do something that is not in line with stated policy. If you want to change or amend anything find out the procedures by which this might happen.

YOUR COLLEAGUES

Your colleagues can be a great source of strength. The cliché 'a problem shared is a problem halved' is often true. Social support is not to be under-estimated in how much better it can make you feel when the going gets tough.

How to recognize your support

- The colleague who regularly smiles at you.

- The one who asks you how it's going.

- The person who speaks well of others behind their backs rather than participates in gossip and slander.

- The colleague who seems to be calm and well-organized; a highly harassed and stressed teacher has little energy left for anyone else.

- The one who offers help: 'Just ask if you need anything'.

The research says that the most likely person to be a buddy is someone at your own level (Hertzog, 2002). Seek out new teachers like yourself, especially those who have a similar and constructive approach to their work.

If you meet anyone who makes it clear they are primarily in it for the long holidays just arrange to meet them for the occasional night out – they are not going to be much help to you in the job, though they may be great fun in the pub!

Supportive colleagues fall into several camps.

Constructive friends

This is someone you feel safe with and with whom you can share some of the difficulties you face. Such a relationship is mutual. If you both admit concerns, mistakes and anxieties you will be able to find ways of supporting each other – the relationship is one of equals.

A constructive friend will not de-skill you by trying to tell you what to do but will listen carefully, help you explore issues and share ideas. They will be empathic but not always take your point of view such as agreeing that the student in question is 'nothing but trouble'. They will help you develop other ways of thinking.

Spending some time in each other's classrooms can be valuable. An observer may see things you don't and be able to suggest ways of changing or adapting what you do. They will also be able to acknowledge your successful strategies and validate your ability. Being in another person's classroom also gives you another learning opportunity. What are they doing that you could usefully incorporate into your own teaching? Sharing resources might also be a possibility.

You need someone to off-load and moan to at times but take care this is not the extent of your conversation, as over time it will bring you both down. Share strategies that you have tried, provide a confidence boost for each other and help develop useful ways of seeing things, such as solution focused thinking.

More experienced colleagues

Try and identify teachers who seem to be enjoying their work, who manage conflict assertively but fairly and who have the respect of students. Do not confuse respect with fear. The teacher who has an air of quiet confidence and self-assurance is the one to look out for. Make a note of the following and check it against the suggestions in Chapter 2.

- Body language – how do they manifest self-confidence?
- In which ways do they gain student attention?
- How do they talk – what is the volume, pitch and tone?
- How do they convey expectations?
- What do they say and not say to students?

Mentors

Many education authorities now assign mentors to new teachers. How well they fulfil this function depends on their individual personality and approach, the training they have had and whether they see their role primarily as an executive supervisory position or a supportive one. Where the role has been imposed rather than voluntary they may be resentful rather than supportive. Others may be angels in disguise with constructive suggestions that make all the difference to your ability to thrive and survive.

School counsellors, educational psychologists and behaviour support teachers

There are several 'behaviour specialists' attached to schools who could be of great help to you in different ways. School counsellors are often on staff in schools in Australia and the United States but this is not so common in the UK. Behaviour support teachers or advisors are sometimes just there to support students but in most instances their brief is also to support teachers. In the UK educational psychologists visit all state schools on a regular basis. Although their time is often spent discussing and assessing pupils with a high level of difficulty, many also see their role as an early intervention consultant. They will be pleased to talk with teachers about issues, rather than named children. This is an effective use of time because it does not entail the need for a parental referral and suggestions for approaches will either make further consultation unnecessary or inform a later assessment. Many educational psychology and behaviour support services also provide training on behaviour and related issues.

All personnel with psychology training know the importance of confidentiality. Unless there is a risk of harm where mandatory reporting is required, you should be able to trust them with your concerns. You can be honest about how you are struggling and not fear they will report you behind your back. If you are in any doubt about this make sure you mention it at the outset of your discussion.

Psychologists have training in listening skills and will help you identify your major concerns and ways to address these. They will not make value judgements or apportion blame but help you think around issues and structure some plan of action. You may find psychologists and counsellors who work with a solution-focused approach rather than a problem based one. There is more on this way of thinking in Chapter 7.

The senior management and executive

These individuals can make a great difference not only to the working lives of new teachers but also of established colleagues. They are the ones in a position to have most impact on policy development, the dominant discourses and consequently on school culture. They range from the school principal who 'was always there for me, always supportive, always helpful' to the deputy headteacher who sees new teachers as incompetent if they need help to enable them to cope. The struggles and trials in those first few months and years are seen as a 'right of passage' – 'I survived through my first years of teaching – they will do the same'.

CASE STUDY

The best of school leaders can have a profound effect on school morale. In one large secondary school the head teacher made a point of finding out about each of his staff as individual people. He showed them that he valued their contribution, both in terms of the work they did and the people they were. He listened as much as he talked but still had a firm hand on the way the school ran. When he returned to school after recovering from a serious illness the staff had decorated the staff room to welcome him back and made cakes in his honour. They rated him highly and loved working in his school.

The support staff

Non-teaching staff can make a significant difference to your life and survival (Morehead, 1998). They include the janitor or caretaker, the school secretary, the people who help out at lunchtime, the classroom assistants. Make a point of acknowledging their value in making your job run smoothly. You would certainly know about it if they weren't there or made it more difficult!

YOU SUPPORTING OTHERS

You might put ideas from this book into place and find they work a treat! Be very careful not to de-skill other colleagues by saying 'But I

We all need to support each other to survive

don't find that class a problem'. Share your solutions in a way that is supportive rather than undermining. This will also contribute to the positive ethos of the school.

CAUSE FOR CONCERN MEETINGS: COLLABORATIVE SOLUTIONS FOR DIFFICULT STUDENTS

'Cause for concern' meetings provide mutual support for teachers, facilitate the sharing of information and help develop consistency for specific students presenting behaviour which is difficult to understand and/or respond to effectively. They are a way of generating ideas for management and meeting needs. Hanko (1999) outlines the benefits to professional competence and well-being of working in collaboration with colleagues.

If such meetings are not happening in your school you may like to discuss the possibility of introducing them. If you think that the idea has any chance of getting off the ground speak to the movers and shakers who are most likely to be helpful.

Cause for concern meetings need to be constructive and solution-focused, not a moaning and labelling session or a strategic pre-requisite to exclusion. The following may be helpful as a basic framework.

- Explore what makes these students difficult to teach, including both the pupil's behaviour and the teacher's perception of this and their responses.

- Talk about all the feelings involved and how these impinge on what the student does and what the teacher does.

- Acknowledge the difficulties of management while accepting the professional responsibilities to meet needs.

- Check what has been tried that has had any positive effect and may be worth building on.

- Consider the need for 'reframing' – looking at the situation differently.

- In which ways are parents involved? Are there better ways of doing this?

- Check what resources are available to teachers, including their own strengths.

- Brainstorm ideas.

- Agree to put one or more of these in place.

- Agree when to review.

NEGATIVE AND UNHELPFUL COLLEAGUES

Sadly, some people you work with can potentially make your life a misery – possibly much more than the students. Such people can use up your emotional resources and drain your enthusiasm for teaching quicker than anything. They may also undermine your chosen approach in your class. You need to know how to survive these colleagues as much as you do the students!

These people might be in positions of seniority in relation to you and you will need to think carefully about how you are going to respond. As with being prepared to deal with children who present difficulties, you need to think about how to defend yourself against the onslaught of negativity from adults.

Colleagues who cause most heartache and self-doubt are those who have their own personal agendas and have not learnt how to be constructive. They

- focus almost exclusively on problems

- write negative, unconstructive comments

- ignore what you have done well and only comment on deficits and difficulties

- rarely say anything positive about other people

- are self-absorbed

- do not ask you what you think

- are cynical about new ideas

- pick new ideas to pieces

- lack creativity

- talk about students in terms of labels rather than strengths and qualities

- demonstrate a value system that is judgmental and exclusive – for example, they may only value 'bright' children

- think that anything but an authoritarian approach is a soft option

- show little interest in others at a personal level

- show little understanding of emotional literacy

- are bossy, bullying or pedantic.

Power issues may be involved. This includes the formal power invested in management but also the informal power in the school. The person who is most influential might be the one who rubbishes everything that is suggested. You know the sort of thing: raised eyebrows, looking around for supportive colleagues, asides and weighty silences.

What do you do about negative and unhelpful colleagues?

As with the students who cause you difficulty, the first thing you need to do is to think differently. You can choose one or more of the following constructions.

Disengage Decide that this person is not going to undermine your sense of self. Learn from Buddhist practice and disengage emotionally. You can't ignore someone entirely without being rude and playing them at their own game but you can interact at the minimum level. As with students you need to maintain professional and personal integrity. This means that you are polite, behave according to your own values and principles but otherwise duck out of confrontation. If this person is someone with whom you have to work closely then this will be more difficult. When things get really bad imagine yourself in a film and step outside yourself to watch the interaction. This helps protect you emotionally and you will be able to handle difficulties in a calmer way.

Be empathic Some individuals have a miserable take on life. They may not have much fun at home or much satisfaction at work. They may be threatened because you are perhaps younger, more attractive, more energetic, more popular, more able, more well-adjusted or simply have your future ahead of you. Saying anything nice is just going to unbalance the situation even further. They may need to get one over you in order to feel good about themselves. What a shame they can't do this any other way. Politely give them space and distance.

Grin and bear it, and look for a way out If you are isolated in your school with no-one to support you, then think hard about whether or not to change schools. Don't leave the profession, there are some lovely people out there.

Bullying and harassment

If someone is in an executive position of authority over you and is behaving in ways that are unacceptable, keep a written and dated account of interactions. In this way you have some evidence of bias should you be in a position of needing a reference and prefer to go over their head to get it. Have others present in meetings where you are being 'called to account'.

If you haven't done it already join your professional association. You never know when you might need them.

A SAFE HAVEN

You need somewhere in school where you can relax, be yourself and not feel intimidated. If your staffroom is not psychologically safe somewhere else in school might be – a supportive colleague's classroom perhaps. A safe haven is somewhere where it is possible to admit mistakes and ask for help without fear of ridicule, either covert or overt. Where conversation is warm, inclusive and friendly, where students are discussed with real concern and attempts made to understand the difficulties that families might be having then the environment is unlikely to be threatening. Where people talk about others, whether they be students, families or colleagues in terms of blame and derision this raises the possibility that everyone will be a potential target. Seeking out your safe haven will help your survival.

SUMMARY

Much has been written about effective schools. We know that a healthy culture is central but that this is subtle and often difficult to define. Effective schools appear to be 'learning organizations', are inclusive and value individuals throughout the system. For new teachers this means, amongst other things, colleagues who offer constructive advice and support as well as positive feedback. For students it means structures which provide for caring as well as high expectations for attainment.

Chapter 6

You and the Community

Your school will be situated within a community and your students will bring that community with them into school. If, as a new teacher, you avoid making assumptions about students you have more chance of being in touch with the young people you teach. This will impact on your ability to establish and maintain good relationships with them and with their families.

It is easy to make assumptions without realizing it. What has been important to you in your life, or is important to the education department, may not be shared by the families in your school. They may have other concerns and priorities.

If you come from a family where education is valued, where you had a room in which to do homework, where getting it done was not dependent on whether your father was sober or not, where you had access to books and computers and girls were considered equal with boys you will begin with an image of your students lives which may be far from their daily experience and reality. You may have supportive parents who value you for who you are, rather than what you do. Some families are so keen on educational achievement that the pressure on young people not to fail becomes overbearing. This impacts both on individual students and their teachers. Not every student can be an outstanding 'success'.

Community awareness does not mean lowering expectations of students but finding out enough about them to tune into their specific needs and to have some idea of what you might put in place to maximize outcomes. It helps you have a better understanding of why students do or do not take up the role of 'good student'. It will also illustrate how much school culture determines what this should be and how those individuals who are unable or unwilling to conform are constructed.

WHAT DOES COMMUNITY MEAN?

For the purpose of this book community includes

- the various cultures that the school serves
- their history, language, values, priorities and expectations
- the relationships within and between the various cultures
- levels of safety and security in the neighbourhood
- the educational resources available both within families and those provided by local services, such as libraries and internet access
- availability and accessibility of other resources such as transport, interpreter services, child-care, community support, etc.

COMMUNITY CULTURE

The best place to find out about the various communities your school serves is from your students. In Chapter 4, It was emphasized that making the curriculum relevant to students raises the likelihood of their engagement. Building your investigations into lessons shows interest and respect.

Find out from your students what your community cultures have to say about

- food
- festivals
- family
- clothing

- having fun

- music

- tradition and rituals

- religion

- hospitality.

CONFLICT OF VALUES

You may feel that your values and those of the community are not the same, such as the positioning of women. This can be hard to deal with. First, check out carefully any assumptions you might have made; you may be surprised to find more similarity than you expected. Secondly, find out how individuals see themselves. It is easy to fall into the trap of stereotyping. Imagine how you might feel if everyone pre-judged your values on the basis of what they understood was typical of your race, gender, religion, sexuality or skin colour.

Where you do find differences you do not have to change your values to accommodate others but if you are overly critical you may lose the confidence of the community. It is a question of combining integrity with sensitivity. This means choosing what to say and when to say it rather than being outspoken with your views. Taking a stance of curiosity and asking respectful questions tends to lead to more fruitful interactions than making statements.

HISTORY

A big issue for non-English-speaking communities will be their recent history. Many families will have experienced disruption and some severe devastation. Children who have witnessed violence, even murder, and lost close relatives in war zones will not necessarily find it easy to adapt to the expectations and routines in school. Considering the struggles many families have been through, it is to their credit that most children settle well into school. Some students, however, will have been seriously affected by their experiences and this may cause you and them difficulty in the classroom. Conversations with families will help you put children's behaviour into context and may give you ideas about how it makes sense to them. Ask the family how they are handling things themselves and identify the support they are receiving. This is a start in deciding how best to respond in the classroom.

MOBILITY

Some schools have a high level of mobility in their student population. Students settle in and are then gone again with others taking their place. Some mobility is by choice but much is caused by circumstances. Mobile students include asylum seekers, those in temporary accommodation, families experiencing breakdown or escaping violence, traveller families and those where parental work commitments involve moving around a great deal. Student mobility contributes to interrupted education and therefore poor access to the curriculum. It is unsurprising that it is also associated with higher levels of absenteeism and behavioural difficulty (Wormington, 2002).

These are some ways in which the needs of mobile and vulnerable students might be addressed.

- Formal peer support systems for incomers so that they learn the ropes quickly and have a small group who are responsible for their social well-being in the first couple of weeks (Newton and Wilson, 1999).

- Assistance with uniform including a list of agencies who may be able to fund basic items; refer to your home school liaison officer.

- Assessment of learning, especially literacy, so appropriate expectations can be made and programs put in place without delay. If possible, request reports from the previous school and check whether formal procedures to assess any special educational needs have been initiated.

- Flexibility and understanding that students will not necessarily know or be able to conform to all the rules and regulations. This simply requires reminders and gentle reinforcements of expectations.

CASE STUDY

Charlene's family had been on the move for several years, one step ahead of her father who had a history of violence. The family now had some respite as her father had received a custodial sentence. Charlene was keen on school, especially as she was receiving extra help with her reading, but all the moving around meant she had to get two buses to school and public transport was unreliable. One morning Charlene's first bus did not turn up on time and she missed the second. She arrived to school very late. The senior teacher who shouted at her as she walked through the door did not realize how much he frightened her. Charlene decided that if there was any small chance she might be late she would come home instead as it was safer. The home liaison officer took several weeks to persuade Charlene – and her understandably protective mother – that she would not get into trouble for lateness and that it was better for her to come late than not at all. Getting the senior teacher to agree also took time.

CONTINUING STRUGGLES

Some communities find themselves the target of continuing racism. Racist attitudes and behaviour can be subtle but very undermining for those who are faced with it. It is easy to stereotype, criticize and condemn. If we are to work effectively with communities we need to examine our own prejudices and see if these are impacting on how we relate to children and their families. Do we for instance, consider the dominant culture to be the 'right' one, the one to aspire to and others as somehow deficient? Are 'white' communities seen as the norm and non-white as the 'outsiders'? Do we assume that because someone doesn't speak our language that they are unable to understand? Do we impose what we think is 'good' for a family rather than make decisions together? Racial inequality is multi-faceted and deeply embedded in Western societies and we all need to be aware of how this impacts on our interactions as teachers (Diniz, 2002). As a new teacher you will have limited influence on the way your school responds to community issues but you can take responsibility for your own interactions. What you do will impact on your relationship with families and pupils. This is one place where students can teach you – encourage and empower them to do so.

TWO-WAY COMMUNICATION

Families in the community may have very different experiences and expectations of education. Some will have little formal education and not had the opportunity to become literate in their own language, let alone a second one. This will have considerable impact on their confidence, especially in meeting teachers. Where education has been a rare or valued commodity in their country of origin the opportunities provided by the host countries may be of great importance. Some communities have high aspirations for their children where others may not see the relevance of the education system. Some parents want the education system to replicate the more formal systems they have left behind and may not put a high value on informal, creative or collaborative activities. They therefore need the purpose of these explained. Giving information to parents about what you are doing in the classroom and why is often helpful in getting family support. Making a video or a photographic display of children carrying out specific activities in the classroom is a good way to communicate this and also develops pride in your students.

Asking parents to share some of their own expertise is also helpful and respectful. This can be anything from teaching children's games to cookery to telling stories to children in their own language.

You can also show your interest in your students' lives by going to some community festivals and events. Not only might you have a great time, you will forge a stronger link with both your students and their families.

POTENTIAL CONFLICT FOR STUDENTS

For some students there is an inherent conflict between what their own family considers important and what the school considers important. Sometimes they have to make hard choices.

Tommy came from a large extended family, notorious in the neighbourhood for alcohol abuse and pub brawls. The police were forever knocking at their door for something or other. Tommy was out of mainstream school because he was hardly ever there and was rude to teachers when he was. In the small special class in which he was placed he began to build positive relationships with the staff. In time he began to see where learning could lead and to want things for himself. His uncle and older brothers, however, had other ideas and began to berate and belittle him for his interest. He was made to feel an outsider in his own family.

Adrian came from an academic family – both his parents were teachers and one taught at university. His younger sister regularly came home with glowing reports from school. Adrian, however, was not the academic type and only did well with practical subjects. A couple of teachers regularly expressed their disappointment with him in comparison to the rest of his family. Even though his family did not put pressure on him to be like the rest of them, Adrian was made to feel like an outsider at school. He left with little formal qualifications but now runs his own successful business.

STUDENT CULTURE

Find out what is available in the neighbourhood: libraries, clubs, sporting facilities. Where do the teenagers hang out together and how safe is the neighbourhood? All of these things impact on students in school.

You may find it useful in your communication with students if you make the effort to watch a TV program popular with young people – perhaps a soap. It gives you a connection with them, another point of showing interest and even something to build into lessons. Try to understand why they like it!

MEETING WITH PARENTS AND CARERS

New teachers often feel anxiety in meeting up with the parents of their students, especially when there are difficult things to talk about. They fear parents will be demanding, even aggressive and threatening. The natural response is to go on the defensive. This is unlikely to have a positive outcome. It is also easy to jump to conclusions about how much families care and quickly blame them for their child's difficulties. Where families have inappropriate or harmful parenting practices it is essential you work with them as constructively as possible (Harskamp, 2002). The following framework for interaction may help (Roffey, 2002).

Communicate positive messages with all parents about their children, but especially about those individuals who are causing you the most trouble. This can be via written communication, a verbal comment when parents deliver or collect their child, at more formal parent-teacher consultation or a 'well done for . . .' certificate that the student can share at home. Such positive home-school communication has two outcomes. Parents are more likely to make the effort to see you when there is a problem and they will be less defensive when they are there.

When you do want to see parents about individual students, keep things at a low level as much as you can. Tell parents you need their help and want to hear their views on their child. Respect their parental role – it may be that no-one else does. You may disagree fundamentally with how a family is bringing up their children but if you bear in mind that most parents want the best for their children and do the best that they can with the knowledge, skills, resources and support that is available to them you may be slower to condemn what you consider to be inappropriate parenting.

CASE STUDY

Mai-Ling was often bad-tempered and moody. She also put little effort into her work and seemed tired and apathetic. Her parents had not attended regular parent-teacher consultations so a note was sent home to ask them to come into school. They did not respond. Further investigations discovered that they could not read or write English. The local community association was contacted and helped arrange an appointment for them in school with an interpreter. In this meeting the circumstances finally became clear. The family worked every night in their own restaurant to try to make a good living for themselves and their daughter. Mai-Ling was with them and often did not get to bed until the restaurant closed. They thought they were doing their best and did not realize how much this was affecting their daughter's education. With the school and the community association they began to look at possible solutions.

For more formal meetings ask a parent to bring a friend with them. Let them know that this is routine practice. This reduces feelings of isolation, provides someone to talk to after the meeting and perhaps take a share in looking after younger children who accompany the family. It is hard for parents who may be emotionally distraught to hear everything that is said.

Focus any discussion on the needs of the child, not the needs of other students, nor your own management needs. You are not there to convince the parent that their child is a walking nightmare and you have thirty other students to think about. A list of misdemeanours will either make the parent clam up with embarrassment, go into defensive mode and perhaps get angry with you or agree with everything you say leaving the child with no advocate at home or at school.

Find out from parents their view of their child and their needs. This will help paint the fullest picture and help 'co-construct reality' rather than fight for different views of the child to take precedence.

Make decisions jointly rather than tell parents what you want them to do. This takes account of what is possible for them to do to help. Many parents want to be seen as supportive but cannot follow through what they have agreed.

Encourage parents to have a positive view of their child and what they might do to reinforce strengths and competencies. This makes a difference to parent–child relationships and parental confidence. Where parents have the view that their child can do no wrong, do not spend valuable energy into trying to persuade them differently. Applaud their loyalty and continue to focus again on the needs of the student in school.

Family breakdown

Sometimes parents do not realize the impact of family breakdown on their children or are too embarrassed or upset to talk to them about it. Children may be confused and feel a sense of loss. This is often expressed as anger in school. It is particularly hard for younger ones who frequently believe it is their fault (Dowling and Gorell Barnes, 2000). They need to be reassured of their own worth, that the remaining parent will not leave as well and about what happens now. Probe gently to see if the student is experiencing this situation and without inducing guilt help the parent to understand what their child might be feeling and what their needs are. Suggest they talk to each other.

SUMMARY

Students bring the expectations, values, understanding and priorities of their community with them into the school. The community may be mono-cultural or made up of several cultures. Find out about the cultures within the community that the school serves. What is important to people? What resources are available in the community that will support you and your students? When you are concerned about an individual student, work in collaboration with parents as much as possible to find solutions that make sense to all of you.

Chapter 7

You and Your Biggest Challenges

Your class organization is well in hand, you are looking after yourself, are on top of the teaching and getting on well with both the students and your colleagues. But you are having a continuing struggle with some of the students. It might be that you are a temporary teacher and have not had a chance to develop the classroom ethos to underpin acceptable behaviour. This is an emergency situation. These are some of the behaviours you might find yourself having to deal with.

- Rudeness and insolence.

- Confrontational defiance.

- Aggressive, intimidating or occasionally violent behaviour.

- Psychological bullying, smirking, whispering, finger pointing.

- Taunting and wind-ups.

- Demanding, attention-seeking behaviour.

- Swaggering, swearing, racist and sexist attitudes.

- Impulsive and distracted behaviour.

- High levels of distress in students.

- Apathy, work refusal or avoidance.

- Lying, cheating and denial.

- Students who 'gang up'.

This list probably makes you want to duck out of teaching now! The good news is that the hardest situations are by no means an everyday reality in most schools and there are ways of thinking and acting that help you survive the toughest pupil and the worst situation. Once you have made even a little progress with your most challenging student, your courage, confidence and self-efficacy will all increase and it won't seem so bad as a future prospect. You are armed with ideas and emotional strength.

So what do you do? If you have not had the chance to check out the rest of this book, do so now. Reading this chapter alone will be useful but the foundations need to be in place for the best effect. Otherwise it is like trying to run a marathon before you are fit. You may have a particular intuition about what to do and be successful, but equally you may try ideas suggested here and wonder why they have a limited impact. You also need ways of coping with the tough times so you are not overwhelmed.

Part A of this chapter gives an overview on ways of thinking about behaviour in school and students who present behaviour that is hard to manage. The way you think determines the way you react.

Many say it is issues from home that are the root of students' unacceptable behaviour and it is not the responsibility of a teacher to deal with this. Although understandable, this view does not help you do the job, let alone succeed in it. Whatever pupils bring can either be exacerbated by what happens in school or addressed and modified. Challenging behaviour may not disappear altogether but what you do does make a difference – one way or the other. Being on the side of making things better is in your interests as well as theirs.

You may meet students who do everything they can to be seen as 'hard cases'. This can be intimidating and even frightening. On the surface the effing and blinding might appear to be directly aimed at you but it is more likely to be the result of overwhelming emotions for the individual who doesn't care who is at the receiving end. If you believe that students have it in for you personally you undermine your own chances of survival. If, however, you respond with integrity and emotional intelligence, knowing that the real distress is emanating from elsewhere, you will provide a protective shield for yourself and the possibility of maintaining a constructive relationship with the student.

Individuals should not be allowed 'to get away with things' that are simply unacceptable in the classroom but defensive reactions are not useful. A thoughtful, confident and consistent response enhances your personal and professional integrity, preserves your credibility and may also improve relationships.

Part B is on the important link between learning and behaviour. This is often overlooked and can be crucial. Here we outline a range of learning needs, some of the associated behaviours and some brief guidance on what you might do. Read also the paragraph on differentiation in Chapter 4: You and Your Class.

Part C provides ideas for action where student behaviour or situations are challenging. These ideas are based on a mix of interactive, constructivist and solution-focused thinking, with some behaviourism thrown in. These are far more useful and less energy-depleting than trying to make an individual see the error of their ways and making them do what you want! You are not expected to be a counsellor, that is not your role – but some basic skills that counsellors use can be very useful to you.

IMMEDIATE MANAGEMENT AND LONGER TERM CHANGE

Responses to challenging behaviour are two pronged. The first is how to manage difficulties when they occur. When someone is refusing to do what you are asking or is abusive and defiant in your lesson what do you do?

The second is how to impact on this situation in the longer term. How can you meet this student's needs to help them settle into the class, feel happier about being there and learn? Some teachers concentrate only on the immediate management. This leads to constant reinvention of the wheel when the same situation happens again and again.

It is crucial that your short-term responses to manage difficult situations are congruent with what might be done to develop more appropriate behaviour in the future. You can easily undermine relationships, motivation and support through negative and inappropriate management. This chapter looks at how to avoid this.

Longer-term change does not happen overnight. There is no quick fix. It is not the one-off program or heavy sanction that makes the difference but the clarity of expectations, choice, consequences and consistency of daily positive responses. It is about relationships that take time to develop, exploring what these behaviours might mean for the student and looking for leverage in supporting change. Teachers who manage this with confidence have less of a struggle and are more effective in the classroom than those who pathologize and marginalize children as 'disordered' or resort rapidly to blame, shame, sanctions and sarcasm.

Finally, Part D explores ways to maintain your own personal and professional integrity and emotional resources in the face of seemingly intractable difficulties. How do you keep your head above water and not dread Mondays when some of the students seem intent on giving you hell?

PART A – THINKING ABOUT STUDENTS WITH CHALLENGING BEHAVIOUR

Students who don't 'fit' the system

The education systems in which we work have similar goals for everyone. It is possible that great strengths are lost because of an insistence on a 'one size fits all' provision. Some of the greatest men and women, such as Einstein, did not shine at school because their abilities lay in a specific direction. One Nobel Prize winner nearly didn't get to university at all because he had not been able to pass a language exam. Someone created some flexibility in the system and ultimately let his specific talents shine. There are many stories of individuals classed as 'behaviour problems' in school who had creative or entrepreneurial skills that gave them great acclaim in later years.

Many of our most challenging students who do not 'fit the system' have experienced rejection, loss, abuse or other disadvantages. For some this is a temporary situation, for others this has been their whole lives. Responses to their experiences often lead children to behave in ways considered unacceptable in school, which then reinforces rejection and disadvantage. This spiralling cycle of social exclusion can either be set in stone in school or broken by a different approach. It may be that for some of our children there is nowhere else to make a difference. This section expands on what a 'different approach' might mean and how to put this into operation.

Do you label students *as* problems or see them as young people *with* problems?

Teachers may see their role as attempting to fit these square pegs into round holes – a difficult and thankless task. Trying to make others fit our expectations is rarely easy and it becomes a battle of wills, the struggle for power and control. The alternative is not to condone unacceptable behaviour but to create flexibility in the system to acknowledge strengths and qualities and celebrate the individuality of each student. Holding on to a view of pupils as whole people, with qualities as well as quirks will enable you to find those elements you can work with. Seeking out the glimpses of good and re-conceptualizing students in terms of their competencies and resources will help. There is a meaning to everyone's behaviour, even if we cannot initially make much sense of it ourselves.

CASE STUDY

On Sunday, 11-year-old Matthew spent the day with his dad, who had recently been separated from his mum. Together the two of them made jam and spent the evening delivering pots as gifts to friends and neighbours. When Matthew got home late his mum was angry with him and with his dad because his homework wasn't finished. Matthew went to bed feeling confused and upset. On Monday, he was suspended from school for an episode of violence when he banged a classmate's head deliberately against a wall.

The behaviour was unacceptable and sanctions were appropriate, but labelling Matthew as 'violent, cruel, a bully or a monster' puts him in a position which offers little escape. It acknowledges only one aspect of who he is as a person and looks to him to do all the changing. It also provides for self-fulfilling prophecies. We all tend to live up to the labels we are given. Reframing Matthew's behaviour as a sign of distress paints a different picture of him. He can be said to be behaving like a

CONTINUED

monster but if he is acknowledged as a person rather than a problem there are things to build on. In all interactions with students it is essential to make it clear that it is their behaviour that is unacceptable – not them. Acknowledging the 'whole person' also makes it easier to work with families (see Chapter 6: You and the Community).

Do you see children as monsters or behaving like monsters?

Focusing on solutions rather than problems

We have a problem-saturated society. Positives often get submerged. When we try to identify positives people often seem to prefer to jump back into negativity. They are not used to doing it! One of the fastest growing movements in school psychology is solution-focused thinking. This switches conversations around to a different focus. If we were dealing with a challenging student a solution-focused approach would ask questions such as.

- What is working well?

- When do difficult things *not* happen?

- What are the circumstances of any positives – for example, with which teacher or adult is the behaviour most appropriate? What is this person doing that seems to work?

- Does this student have any supportive relationships?

- What strengths does this student have – in anything?

- What are they are able to manage?

- What have they learnt?

- What helps them cope?

- What comforts them and makes them feel better?

- What helps them calm down?

- What has worked well in the past?

- What can this student be proud of?

- How does the student visualize life without the problem?

- What can we build on here?

- What can we put in place so the student knows they are being successful, being supported, being valued?

- What would the student see as solutions for themselves. They might be the only person to know what the real options are (Berg and Steiner, 2003).

Thinking about behaviour itself

Behaviour only has meaning within a context. There is virtually no behaviour that does not have an appropriate context somewhere. Screaming and yelling is what you are supposed to do at a big match if your team scores. Screaming and yelling in the classroom is seriously frowned upon. What we are talking about is often a mismatch between the behaviour we require from students and the behaviour they bring with them.

It helps students to succeed at school if they are taught in a structured and supportive way what is appropriate behaviour in a classroom. They also need to know what is not acceptable and why. In the first place it may be more constructive for teachers to assume ignorance rather than defiance. This is particularly important for transitions into a new school or new class (Roffey and O'Reirdan, 2001).

Sitting still and writing, not talking, obeying school rules, wearing the 'right' uniform and so on are not about being 'good' but being part of a social order. These behaviours have no moral quality, neither are they particularly 'natural' for lively young people. Expectations are on pupils to ensure a controlled environment. Most students take up this position of being a 'good student' in the same way as you take up the behaviours of what you understand to be a 'good teacher'. It is worth acknowledging here that students in fact have few real choices. Even though sometimes we offer choices and consequences to maintain 'appropriate' school behaviour these are controlled by the power of the institution. Acknowledging this may help us to see how much even the most defiant students accept what is required of them, even if they don't manage it sometimes.

School demands and expectations do not always make sense to some students and may undermine their need for a sense of agency. If they have little choice over much that happens in their lives they are going to try and control what they can. If we work with this understanding then we have other avenues of response that are more honest and respectful. This may have a more positive outcome for all involved.

The meaning of behaviour for students

Sometimes it seems as if the education system is only interested in measurement and little is done to find out what is meaningful. When it comes to behaviour in school, however, it is often useful to have some idea of what certain actions mean for students. Many behaviours, for instance, can be interpreted as 'coping mechanisms'. Meanings are often hidden, not deliberately but because the triggers are deeply buried in past experiences.

CASE STUDY

> One young girl displayed difficult behaviour with one male teacher only – and only at certain times. For a long time no-one could understand why. Careful analysis revealed that the distressed behaviour only occurred on days he was wearing a blue check shirt. It was then discovered that the girl's abusive father, with whom she no longer lived, used to wear a similar shirt. The teacher wearing a blue check shirt brought back painful memories of home that triggered emotional upset. When he stopped wearing the shirt the behaviour improved.

Sometimes it requires only a good relationship, a suspension of prejudice and a moment of listening to have a way of understanding. Being prepared to do so may be linked to how the student is positioned by the school in the first place. The following anecdote was written about a student, Shane, who had been labelled as a 'behaviour problem' and who was being reintegrated from special education into a mainstream school. Cath is his special school principal.

Shane was suspended from his regular school today. In assembly he was wearing his baseball cap. When he was asked to take it off he refused, got up, turned his back on the principal, said nothing and walked out in front of a couple of hundred students. Shane was suspended for this action. Shane later told Cath that he had had his hair cut short and did not want it seen – but of course he could not say that at the time. To provide such an explanation in front of the assembly would be embarrassing. His action was read as powerful and disruptive. The staff at school were extremely upset by his refusal to comply and perhaps even a little afraid of what they saw as his challenge . . . It is our observation that if Shane had often displayed good student behaviours and if he had been recognized by staff as one who displayed them there is a good chance that his wearing of a hat in assembly would not have been read as bad behaviour (Honan et al, 1998). It would have been assumed that he had good reasons for wearing a hat (i.e. that he was a rational human being) even though these reasons might not be immediately visible.

(Laws and Davies, 2000)

Psychological survival is a motivation for many behaviours, and underpins emotions that are associated with fear and defence. Young people who have had difficult experiences may construe the world as a hostile place and see demands, expectations and social interactions as potentially threatening. No-one needs to tell you to eff-off unless they interpret what you are asking as a threat. We live in a society that is increasingly based on competition, fear of failure and wariness of others. This may account in part for the numbers of young people who need to protect their sense of self by whatever means is at hand. Making an effort to understand what a student's behaviour means for them gives us more chance of working together to change it.

You can help to discover meanings by looking at patterns in behaviour, by talking to children about the pictures they draw, sometimes just by asking indirect and open questions and listening – for example, 'You seem a bit bothered lately, what's up?'. You may only get a useful answer if the student feels safe with you and does not feel interrogated. It works better if you are doing something together, like tidying up or walking around the playground rather than in a face-to-face encounter.

Should you find yourself in a situation where a student discloses abuse you must make it clear immediately that you are obliged to tell someone whose job it is to protect children. Check out the child protection procedures in your school and which staff member has responsibility for this.

Sometimes you can 'reframe' behaviour for a student which interprets its meaning in terms of qualities rather than deficits. For example, young students sometimes explode at the taunt 'Your mum is a . . .' even before the sentence is finished! If the student is given credit for loyalty they may then listen to why it is not necessary to punch the perpetrator on the nose!

PART B – THE LEARNING AND BEHAVIOUR CONNECTION: CHECK THIS OUT FIRST

There is a wealth of evidence to show that many children presenting behaviour difficulties in the classroom are struggling with learning (Dearden, 1994; Roffey and O'Reirdan, 2001). They may fall into one or another of these categories.

- They are developing at a slower pace than other students.

- They have a specific difficulty, especially in literacy skills, where they consistently fail to meet the expectations of others.

- They do not understand the language of instruction.

- They have unmet emotional needs or are experiencing great distress which impinges on their ability to learn.

- They are not skilled in paying attention to teacher input and have a fragmented concentration on set tasks.

- They are more able than their peers and either trying to 'fit in' or are under-stimulated in class.

A significant proportion of younger children have intermittent conductive hearing loss. The statement 'she hears me when she chooses to' signals the need for a hearing assessment. In the meantime, make sure you are not in shadow so the pupil can lip-read. Similarly some students have poor vision and are therefore unable to read instructions. Suggest parents take them for a routine eye test.

Students with long term learning needs may have a developmental path that is slower in all aspects. Their behaviour may be seen as inappropriate compared to their peers. It should not take long to identify such students though many are noted for behaviour difficulties long before their learning needs are realized. Such pupils need developmentally appropriate expectations for both learning and behaviour. Ask for assessment and guidance from those in your school who have responsibility for learning support. In the meantime, gather evidence of what the student can actually do so you can build on current knowledge at the appropriate place and pace.

Students who have a specific difficulty in learning, such as a struggle with achieving literacy, may choose to behave in ways which maintain their self-esteem rather than accept the position of 'a slow learner'. These students are often the class clowns or persistent disrupters. They may feel a failure within the class and may also be conscious of failing their family's expectations. These pupils need evidence of progress and acknowledgement of successes in both their area of need and in their areas of strength – whatever these are.

Communication problems are often linked to behaviour difficulties (Dockrell and Lindsay, 2000). If you cannot understand what is going on you are less likely to be able to conform and if you cannot make yourself understood you are likely to become very frustrated. Small children with language delay may end up screaming to get their needs met. Build visual support into communications. Some children have difficulty processing more than one or two pieces of information at a time and do not understand what is expected. Be concise. Break down instructions into clear steps.

Students with concentration difficulties are often labelled as having attention deficit disorder. They may not be meeting curriculum expectations because they are seriously distracted and cannot stay focused on directed tasks. Other things may be on their mind, leading to a fragmented way of dealing with the world. Sometimes children have not been taught how to begin, develop and finish a task – even eating is a grazing activity rather than sitting down at a meal. They may not discriminate between different stimuli and know what to pay attention to. Sometimes these students get into trouble for what they do when not paying attention to directed activities. This requires a focus on the pre-requisites in settling down to work. Give clear, achievable and if necessary very brief tasks, minimize stimuli and show faith in the student's ability to take control of themselves. In the longer term it is important that these students build up a view of themselves as being able rather than tell you 'I can't do that because I have ADD'.

CASE STUDY

11-year-old Ade was observed in two different class settings on the same day. In the first he was expected to work independently on a given task. He spent 85 per cent of his time wandering the room, sharpening his pencil, looking for glue, stopping to see what others were doing and having a laugh over a dropped eraser, ending up with another student under a table. He appeared to have little idea what was involved in independent activity, and seemed not to have the skills to

CONTINUED

do it. He was said to have attention difficulties. Ade was observed in another classroom. This time the teacher directed all activities, asked students questions to ensure they were on task, gave them clear things to do and let them know what 'finished' meant. This time Ade was on task nearly 85 per cent of the time. No problem with attention there.

Unusual behaviour Some students have a specific difficulty that makes it hard for them to relate socially to others. These individuals present as unusual and worrying. Most children enjoy attention but these pupils tend to avoid all social contact, especially eye contact. They may play in a repetitive way with little imagination or prefer to work by themselves on self-motivated projects. The world appears to be a frightening and confusing place for them. These pupils are likely to be on the autistic spectrum and you need to talk to a specialist for detailed ideas about behaviour management. In the meantime

- build in predictability and order

- reduce anxiety by giving clear individual notice of any transitions between activities

- do not attempt to eliminate obsessive or ritualistic behaviour altogether – offer alternatives

- do not insist on collaborative working but support any social interaction.

Sudden deterioration in attainments Sometimes students start to fall behind quite suddenly. Often this is in conjunction with behaviour also deteriorating. Something is happening for this student that is detracting from their ability to stay focused and behave appropriately. Beware unwanted intrusion, but finding out what is going on helps you respond sensitively. Arrange to see the student for a ten-minute listening session. Bear in mind issues related to bullying, friendship, family breakdown or restructuring, conflict, abuse, rejection, violence, bereavement or illness. Talk about how the student is coping. In many instances a supportive, familiar environment can provide a buffer for students in times of exceptional stress. Refer the student on if appropriate.

Able, bored students   Occasionally students play up because they lack stimulation. Extension activities that demand high levels of creativity and analysis should help. Involve such students in developing their own interests and get advice from staff specializing in gifted and talented pupils. Sometimes students fear being more advanced than their peers. A classroom ethos that celebrates difference helps such students as well as those at the other end of the ability spectrum.

PART C – TAKING ACTION

This section explores what you might do to survive in the classroom with your most difficult students. We begin with what is involved in establishing an optimal relationship. This underpins the successful operation of many of the strategies that follow.

We then look at a range of challenging scenarios in the classroom and specific ideas to help you respond to and survive these. It is not possible to outline all the behaviours you might come across but this should give you the underlying principles for good and effective practice.

Developing positive relationships with challenging students

A focus on developing the best possible relationship is both in your interest and that of the student. Do not, however, attempt to do this cynically. Students see through phoniness in a flash. This means you have to be yourself, accept them unconditionally – even if you seriously disapprove of their behaviour – and demonstrate warmth rather than coldness or hostility. Accept that you will be putting in most of the effort and see it as part of the job. A good relationship raises the chance of any strategy or intervention being effective. Students are more likely to respond positively where they feel teachers are genuinely interested in their well-being. Don't expect your efforts to be a panacea – but they will make a difference.

If you are a teacher who has credibility with the group (see Chapter 2: You as a Teacher), relating positively to this student may boost their self-esteem. A good relationship also offers a role model for empathic, socially skilled and emotionally literate behaviours. Having someone 'on their side' provides a 'resilience' factor for the student (Fuller, 1998).

All of the following are helpful in developing good relationships. Don't be too obvious or heavy with any of this or you risk it all backfiring. And remember what was said earlier about being friendly but not a friend and not handing out special favours.

- Greet the student by name and with a smile.

- Show an interest in the student as a person not just a pupil. Do not interrogate or single them out but be prepared to have brief informal conversations about such things as the team they support, any pets they might have and so on.

- See if you can discover anything you have in common, such as music you both like, a TV programme you both watch, a hatred of tomatoes! Sharing bonds people.

- Try hard to find something about them to genuinely like – this may be a tall order but there is almost always something. Their spirit, infectious laugh, the way they decorate their books, the graceful way they move, whatever! Comment about the person themselves rather than something they own.

- Find opportunities to let them know what you like about them.

- Give positive labels, such as 'I need someone with a good memory to take a message to the secretary – Sam, you could be trusted with that'. So now you have a child who begins to think of himself as able and trustworthy – not someone who can't sit still for a second. Tell a pupil she is helpful and that is what she will try and be, but tell her she is never any help at all and that is what you will get.

- Structure 'success opportunities' rather than inevitable failures.

- Comment briefly on absolutely anything that is a positive – 'I can see that you have written your name at the top of the page – that's a start!'

- Give less responsive students a brief warning of an instruction so that they are forewarned. They may then be more ready to comply and can be held up to others as a model if appropriate.

- A nod or a thumbs-up is often effective.

- Do not provide fulsome praise for students with low self-esteem: it does not fit their self-image and will be dismissed. Give brief, factual and specific feedback. Not just 'I like that or 'that's good' but 'I like that because you have . . .' or 'it is . . .' (see also 'Second hand praise' in Chapter 4: You and Your Class).

- Find something to laugh about together – not being serious about yourself works well.

- Be emotionally engaged in interactions. Being calm does not mean being distant. Show the student that their achievements and success matters to you. Blandness can give the impression that you can't be bothered and the student isn't really important.

Good relationships are demonstrated in what you say and how you say it. See the list in Chapter 8 about helpful and unhelpful phrases.

There is no doubt that teachers who show students respect within an authoritative framework have an easier time than those who coerce, blame and deride. Just 'being nice' doesn't work – it has to be in conjunction with consistent boundaries and expectations.

CASE STUDY

Nathan sat in the counsellor's office, his hat pulled down over his eyes. He was about to be suspended yet again. The counsellor probed gently about the incident that had led to this situation. Nathan had given his art teacher a mouthful of abuse. 'It was her – she just hates me. I tried to explain why I was late but she just went for me, she always does. I hate her, she deserved it.' This behaviour is unacceptable in school, everyone agrees. The counsellor asked about other teachers. Did Nathan get on badly with everyone? No, he didn't. 'Mr Perkins is OK, and so is Miss Wright. They don't sigh every time I walk in the door, they ask me to do things, don't tell me. I don't have trouble in their classes.' Nathan was an able student, having some real difficulties at home with his parents splitting up. He had done well in primary school but was now rapidly becoming one of the 'bad' boys and living up to his reputation. The big shame is that he was a talented artist – it was one of his favourite subjects.

CASE STUDY

Costas is 13 years old. A year ago he attempted to stop his Dad from punching his mother by yelling and screaming at him. As his father turned round to confront his son, he collapsed with a heart attack. Costas now lives with guilt as well as depression and anger. He is also bullied at school and called racist names. He has had two long suspensions for swearing and threatening his science teacher. The last thing he did was run out of his class swearing loudly. Costas was asked why he does not have the same behaviour problems in other classes. 'Those teachers know I have problems at home and that I get bullied in school. They talk to me and help me calm down. They understand so I cooperate, it is hard but I try. This teacher yells at me, tells me to get out and blames me when I react to the teasing. I hate him. He does not even listen to what I have to say.'

These two students are from very different schools but their stories are similar. Relationships in schools matter.

What does it mean to listen?

Teachers are often excellent at talking but rarely trained in active listening. This can, however, be very helpful in the establishment and maintenance of good relationships and in the resolution of behavioural issues. There are adults who appear to believe they have the right to all the airspace in a conversation. What students should be doing is listening and taking note of what they are saying because it's for their own good! When it comes to interactions about behaviour this only entrenches bad feelings and a weakened resolve to do things any differently. This is especially true of adolescents. When fear of retribution is the only reason for doing or not doing something there is no incentive to develop problem-solving strategies or self-control.

You don't have the time for listening to individuals when you are in the middle of teaching. Try the following.

In high school 'I want to hear your side of things (what you have to say/how you think about this, etc.) but clearly this is not the right time. When is a good time for you to come and see me?' You negotiate rather than dictate. This may take the heat out of the immediate situation. It also saves face for everyone. The student is more likely to turn up to see you in a calm state if you do not give the impression that they will need to heavily defend their position. It helps if you avoid saying 'I want to talk to you'.

In primary school 'I have to teach the class now but I want to hear what you have to say. Shall we have a chat at lunchtime/at the end of school? Would you like to bring a friend?' This gives the impression immediately that you are accessible and supportive and not about to read the riot act.

Teacher response in the classroom has an impact on every student, not just the one who is challenging. This calm, clear, approach, which models respectful interactions but also deals confidently with difficulties, will have a positive outcome in your class generally.

When the student arrives to see you make them feel welcome. You may also need to make clear your time limits – 'I have to teach in 15 minutes but we can follow up later if need be.' 'I have this lesson free – how long do you think we will need?'

- Ask the student to tell you their version of the 'problem'.

- Give them your full attention and minimal attention to any interruptions. If anyone knocks ask them to come back later.

- Listen without interrupting. Give encouragements such as nodding, and saying things like 'Go on', 'Explain what you mean', 'Can you say a bit more about that?'

- At appropriate times check and summarize – 'So, what you are saying is . . .'

- Include an acknowledgement of the feelings involved. 'I guess that you are feeling . . . – would that be right?'

- Do not insist on the student answering the question 'why?' Most of the time there is not a straightforward answer and the student may just come up with the last thing that happened. It may, however, be worth asking, what they were thinking or intending at the time. Try not to make a value judgement here.

- Ask the student what they would like to happen now. The student may well come up with things that are not possible. Explain why and ask for other ideas. It may be that the student will want other people to change. Point out that the only people we can have any control over is ourselves. You could, however, say you will follow up concerns of abusive behaviour perpetrated by others.

- Once you have genuinely listened you are at the point when you can address what you need yourself from this student in terms of behavioural change. It is timely to ask 'what do you think you might do/need to make this situation better?' Use a solution focus as outlined above to identify and build on competencies and strengths.

If you run out of time ask the student to think about these last questions and arrange for them to come back. A thinking space might also help.

If students need to talk about serious issues that are happening in their lives and which are impacting on school you may need to refer on, gaining the appropriate permissions.

Your efforts in being approachable and in respectful listening are likely to make a considerable difference to how well this student manages in your own classes in the future. You might think it is time-consuming but compared with alternatives, it is probably a much more efficient use of your time.

Dealing with challenging situations

The key is to find ways of managing challenging situations that at best support a more positive sense of self for the student and at worst do not damage relationships. Some management strategies just exacerbate the difficulties for both the teacher and the student. The aim here is to maximize the possibility of survival for both. This leaves the way open for supporting the development of longer-term changes. In all interactions in challenging situations emphasize that is the behaviour that is unacceptable, not the student.

Dealing with a high level of emotion

CASE STUDY

Hugh is an eight-year-old who was referred to the school counsellor for violence, swearing and anti-social behaviour. He had posed a challenge to the school in his resistance to interventions. The teacher had been to the school counsellor for consultation and on the basis of a new way of thinking had changed her approach.

Hugh got angry with a group of boys who teased him. He swore and started kicking rubbish bins around. The teacher intervened. 'I know that you are angry because things did not go right for you but you can deal with it, Hugh.' The student looked up and the teacher said again, 'Yes, I'm sure you can do it, just come to me when you are ready to continue the lesson.' To the teacher's amazement, Hugh disappeared into the toilet and came back after ten minutes. He said, 'Sir, I'll clean up the mess,' and took the dustpan and brush and cleaned up. The surprised and pleased teacher thanked and rewarded Hugh for being responsible.

We are quite scared of emotional outbursts. In an informal survey of teachers on an in-service-training course, dealing with strong emotions is what bothered them most. They were very unsure about what to do when students exploded in some way.

These explosions can stem from frustration, fear, intrusion, injustice or responses to perceived criticism or rejection. The stress related to the outburst may have been building up for some time. Anger is part of a grief response and is sometimes related to a serious loss in a young person's life. Family breakdown may be more devastating for children than parents realize and school is often a safer place to express these powerful and confusing feelings.

Strong reaction is often triggered by perceived insults, criticism or rejection. Check whether other students are involved in this and address their behaviour if necessary. If you consider this student is 'over-reacting' do not say so but bear in mind that they are interpreting what has happened on the basis of past experiences. Acknowledge their distress but offer alternative ways of seeing what happened.

CASE STUDY

> Catherine was re-integrating from a special school into a mainstream school. Her supportive mother had told her she was as good as anyone else and encouraged her independence. Whenever other students offered help, Catherine interpreted this as a reflection on her learning difficulties and responded accordingly. She constantly scowled at everyone and was becoming increasingly socially isolated. A conversation with Catherine and her mother was helpful and Catherine was encouraged both at school and at home to think about the other students differently.

The manifestations of emotional distress are clenched and taut bodily postures, shouting, crying, stamping, screaming, swearing, throwing and destroying things. Swearing and verbal abuse are common but physical attack less so – usually it is the furniture that gets kicked. This is indicative of at least some level of self-control.

There is a common tendency to negate emotion in some way, either by trying to cheer people up or telling them they are over-reacting and suggesting they 'pull themselves together'. 'Being brave' is given a high value in some cultures especially in males who are not supposed to acknowledge or express fear or distress. Crying is less taboo these days than it used to be, but you still hear people commenting favourably on how well someone 'held up' in difficult circumstances. As a consequence very distressed children, especially boys, often resort to angry outbursts as an alternative to crying. If you closely observe anger you will see that tears are often close to the surface.

This is a framework for responding to anger or other expressions of strong emotion.

- Acknowledge and validate the emotion being expressed.
- Speak quietly and calmly but show concern.
- Show belief in the student's ability to manage their anger or distress.
- Ask what would help the student at the moment – possibly a 'time out'.
- Suggest a place to go.
- Deal confidently with potential dangers.
- If the student continues to be out of control ask another student to go for help.
- When the student has calmed down you can then say that although their anger is something they have a right to, expressing it in that way is not acceptable in school – discuss what they might do in the future.
- Help students tune into warning signs.

A useful first stance is to acknowledge the emotion being expressed: 'I see that you are very upset/angry'. Then validate the emotion so that the student no longer feels she has to continue or even raise the stakes in order for her distress to be 'heard'. Try and listen at an underlying level. The 'trigger' is rarely the root of the emotions. This is likely to be associated with more significant issues.

Primary school students　'Something must have happened to make you so cross today'; 'A good cry might be just what you need'.

Secondary school students　'You must have a good reason for getting so upset.' If you have an idea what has happened you can say, 'It is understandable' or 'I'm not surprised that you feel like that.' Do not say you know how a student feels – you don't, however similar your experience might have been. You can say, 'something like that hap-pened to me and I felt pretty bad about it at the time.' This statement does not make assumptions.

Dealing with outbursts

- Be calm, confident and self-controlled. If you meet anger with anger you will exacerbate it. We tend to mirror the emotions of others. This means that if you are calm and in control of yourself then the student is much more likely to calm down sooner. Keep your voice low, speak slowly and clearly. The student may be more alarmed about their behaviour than you are. It is not a good feeling to have 'lost it'.

- Make reassuring brief statements and show belief in the student. 'It's OK, you will be OK. Take it easy. It's all right. You can deal with this.'

- Offer a 'safe' place – 'Would you like to go outside/to the sick bay/to the office for a while?' The sooner you are able to do this the better, as outbursts provide an interesting diversion for the rest of your class.

- Do not engage in verbal attempts to stop the behaviour except where there is danger and/or potential destruction. Then make direct, calm but very firm requests using 'I' statements and a belief in the student's ability. 'I would like you to put that chair down, please. Put the chair down. You take control here.' The second the student begins to respond positively you thank them, predicting completion. The relationship between you and the student will be a significant factor in whether or not there is compliance.

- Fighting between students needs more assertive action. Address the student who is most likely to comply and tell them firmly and briefly to move away – 'That's enough, Patrick, go and stand by the door – by the door, now, please.'

- If the situation appears to be escalating ask a responsible student to go for assistance. You should know in advance who is the most appropriate staff member to contact.

- You will need to follow up on outbursts in the classroom, especially angry ones. The section above on listening may help to identify what the underlying issues are. Help the student identify alternative ways of expressing their anger or refer them to someone who will assist them in doing this.

It is possible to help students identify their own emotional states and know when they might 'blow'. Using a 'traffic light' system is a way of communicating this to the teacher. A green card on the desk means everything is fine, an orange one means the student is beginning to feel edgy and would like some support, a red one means an explosion is imminent and the student needs permission to take action themselves – such as going and getting a drink to calm down. Fear that students will abuse this intervention is usually unfounded.

A teacher who has 'withitness' (see Chapter 4) will also be able to tune in to the emotional situation and take discreet pre-emptive action themselves.

The following section is also relevant.

Avoiding and managing confrontation

Confrontation is less likely to happen if you have followed the guidelines in the rest of this book, but it does sometimes happen and you need to know what to do and not do. Some things prevent or limit a confrontation while others trigger or exacerbate it. The following framework moves from prevention to inhibition to wise management and limiting escalation.

A positive relationship with a student is your best protection. A history of conflict promotes expectations of yet another. Sometimes conflict has been part of the student's experience throughout their life and this history is out of your control.

Stress levels for both you and the student determine whether a confrontation is more or less likely. Be aware of reducing your stress levels where possible and maximizing your emotional resources. Students might just 'flip' because of what is currently happening in their lives. An otherwise innocuous event in your class might be the last straw.

Focusing on the group rather than singling out an individual in a group situation reduces the chance of confrontation. 'This group seems to be having trouble starting the assignment.' 'Some people seem to be talking about the match rather than getting on with the work.' Giving positive rather than negative attention also helps.

Rhetorical questions and demands for explanations fan the flames of confrontation. 'What do you think you're doing?' can easily be replaced by 'What help do you need here?' Statements that might be interpreted as threats, put-downs or labels are also best avoided. Do not apportion blame.

Demanding that students do something NOW can trigger confrontations. This is usually unnecessary. Make requests and move away giving time for compliance. 'I'll come back in a minute or two and see how you are getting on.' The same applies to giving reminders of instructions before you give reprimands for not getting on with it.

Adult regulation of emotion, appropriate expression and aware body language are all relevant. Avoid anything that might be interpreted as aggressive, such as shouting, interrupting, finger pointing, invading 'personal space' by coming too close: this includes pushing your face forward. Mirroring the body language of the student is the worst thing you can do. Instead keep an appropriate distance, your hands down by your sides, even turn slightly sideways to minimize any perceived threat, use a calm, low voice and employ 'I' statements rather than accusatory 'You' statements.

Keep the interaction as light as you can manage.

Acknowledging feelings addresses one of the potential motivations for the confrontation, denying feelings exacerbates it (see above).

Joining in with the argument and becoming defensive just prolongs the confrontation, gives great entertainment for other students and does your credibility no good at all.

A confrontation is generally a battle of wills so your attempts to assert power and control and put the student in a 'no win' situation are unlikely to work, especially in the longer term. As a teacher you are already in a more powerful position than the student so there is no need to prove this by insisting on 'winning' the showdown. A more emotionally intelligent response is to offer the student some negotiation and face-saving solutions so that you both 'win'. You can do this by offering limited choices and some level of control – 'If you choose to carry on yelling it will have to be reported. If you decide it would be better to talk this over with me later I'd go along with that', 'I am sorry if I gave you the wrong impression. We have clearly misunderstood each other here – but I do need you to calm down so we can sort it out.'

It is crucial that you follow through. It does not maintain your credibility if students see their peers 'getting away' with behaviour which everyone considers unacceptable.

Rudeness

Some students, teenagers in particular, sometimes do not realize how they are coming over. They have body language and facial expressions that can be interpreted very negatively. You will be familiar with the bored look, the slouch and the arrogant sneer. You probably had a selection of such faces and postures yourself once! Other students confuse friendliness with familiarity. A few have not been expected to treat adults any differently from peers. Some have an extensive vocabulary of four letter words that they have learnt to use without discrimination from their earliest days. You need to think hard about what you are going to pay attention to and what you are going to ignore and simply 'not hear'.

If you are in doubt about a specific incident, however, check it out. Ask the student if they intend to be insolent or if they're just upset about something? If they say their intention was to be rude then say that it is unacceptable for them to speak to you in that way and that you do not speak to students in that way. Tell students you are interested in hearing what they have to say but cannot hear past the verbal abuse. Ask them to talk to you in ways that help you understand the issues.

If the student continues to be abusive you could choose to let them exhaust the diatribe without interruption. Bill Rogers in *Classroom Behaviour* (2000) describes how effective it can be to let a student simply 'run out of steam'. You need to be seen by the rest of the class to do this deliberately and be in control of the situation. When the student comes to a significant pause you could simply say, 'Is that all, is there anything else you want to say?' You then offer a time to talk their concerns through in a more appropriate way.

If the student did not intend rudeness then say they could be misinterpreted and get into trouble. Perhaps they need to think about what is acceptable in school because it isn't the same as being with their mates.

Sometimes students are verbally abusive to each other. Make it very clear what is not acceptable in your classroom.

Defiance

Defiance can be described as actively resisting a request or instruction. It comes with the message 'just try and make me!' You might as well agree with that. You cannot make someone do something if they choose not to. What you can do is offer incentives or impose sanctions as consequences. With a good relationship just letting them know you feel let down might be sufficient.

The student is asserting control and power and you could choose to respond to that positively and lightly – 'You know, some of the bravest people in the world didn't do as they were told either, sometimes it takes some spirit and courage, especially if you know you might get executed as a result.' This will reduce the level of emotion in the situation and possibly bring in some humour. You could then say, 'Of course schools don't execute people for not doing as we ask them to but there are consequences.' Then clarify consequences with the student. Continue with 'Well, think for a minute if you want that to happen. If you decide to do as you are asked I will come and check on whether you need any help in a minute.' Walk away and check on someone else.

This leaves you in control of the situation but not controlling the student. It is calm, respectful – and gives clear messages to the rest of the class.

It is possible that the student is unable to do what you have asked or fearful she will fail. If you have a reluctant or defiant student check what levels she is working at. Reward effort as well as success.

Social cruelty

This runs the gamut from mild teasing, to mother cussing, to behaviour that is psychologically damaging. More extreme forms of social cruelty can include intimidation, exclusion, vicious verbal attacks and actual physical harm. It can also include destructive behaviour with damage to other people's work or property. Social cruelty can be perpetrated by individuals but also by groups of students. Even when there is only one student doing this there are almost always others who are onlookers and have a responsibility.

This level of unkindness can really get teachers down. It challenges their values, causes inner conflicts, outrages their sense of justice and makes them feel both angry and helpless.

The answer to social cruelty is to address the issue as a social phenomenon. We now know that work with students labelled bullies and victims has only limited success – anti-bullying measures need to be embedded in whole school structures and practice (Sharp and Smith, 1994). Schools have different ways of doing this – from peer counsellors to bully courts. Circle time sessions are really valuable here (see Chapter 4). They focus on issues rather than individuals and the social responsibility of everyone to support each other. There are details of how to find more about circle time, circle of friends and other anti-bullying strategies in Chapter 8.

⬤ Racism, sexism

Racism and sexism are usually actively addressed in schools. If you come face to face with this behaviour let students know it is unacceptable in your classroom. Tell them what school policies say and give warnings about sanctions. Impose penalties if necessary. You are unlikely to change a person's attitude in the short term – so don't preach as part of your management. If you have credibility with students your own disapproval of racist and sexist behaviour and treating everyone equally in your class will be helpful in changing attitudes over time (see 'Continuing struggles' in Chapter 6: You and the Community).

As with social cruelty peer pressure is central. Use class discussions and curriculum materials to address these issues.

For individuals who continue behaving towards their peers in unacceptable ways let them and others know that you are keeping a record of incidents. This is also useful for anyone who is a target. Give them a notebook. It may stop the behaviour and provides an assertive but non-confrontational strategy.

⬤ Swaggering, swearing, outrageous behaviour and infringing uniform rules

These behaviours are clustered together because they are often part of an 'attitude' within an adolescent peer group. Ignore the swaggering and choose not to hear the swearing unless it is directed at you or someone else. Sometimes it will be deliberately challenging and you have little choice but to address it. A raised eyebrow may be all that is needed or a simple 'not appropriate for school, guys.' For some students it is everyday vocabulary. You might not like it but moral outrage is misplaced. Give the students alternatives if this might be useful or appropriate.

The intention with outrageous behaviour is to confront or shock so avoid both. Lack of the desired response will reduce the behaviour. Reinforce what the school rules say in ways that avoid a confrontation. Much of this will be related to what students are supposed to wear and not wear in school. Uniform issues are the cause of many confrontations between staff and students, especially in secondary education. Infringements of uniform policy are often a way of asserting individuality and taking back some power from the 'system'. Keep your response low-key – 'I love your earrings but you do know that long dangly earrings are not allowed in school? Do you have somewhere safe to keep them when you take them off?'

⬤ Passively resisting instructions or avoiding working

Students who have continual difficulty settling to work can be a chronic problem for teachers. They may have learning difficulties, low self-esteem or be just too pre-occupied to pay attention. What often happens is they become chronic disruptors – rolling under tables, disturbing other students, talking out of turn, getting into trouble generally. Deal with the work issue first and you may already be solving the disruption issue.

Helping students focus

- Check if they know what they are supposed to do.
- Check they are able to do it.
- Ask them to tell you what they should be doing first.
- If necessary, tell them exactly what they are supposed to do – briefly.
- Check they have the equipment they need.
- Do they know where to find what they don't have?
- Start the task with them if necessary.
- Give them a chance to get on with it themselves.
- Don't stand over them.
- Look for and reinforce partial completion: 'Well done, I can see that you have . . .'
- Use verbal and visual prompts to stay on task.

CONTINUED

- Assign a working partner with clarity about who does what.

- Give positive feedback on both effort and achievement.

See 'Personal bests' in Chapter 4.

Impulsive behaviour

For some students the 'thinking gap' between impulse and action is almost non-existent. Any intervening evaluation of potential consequences appears to be missing. This leads pupils into all sorts of scrapes with outcomes they didn't really mean and come almost as a surprise. Impulse control is developmental and you would expect older students to be able to manage better than younger ones. Talk about training their 'brain brakes' to be more effective as they grow up.

A useful way of dealing with impulsivity is to 'externalize' the 'problem' so the student starts thinking about ways of becoming more in control of themselves (Winslade and Monk, 1999). Talk about the student's hands, feet or mouth getting them into trouble and how they are going to take charge of these 'out of control' body parts. Work out where they already have control and build on this. Demonstrate trust in their ability even when impulsive events happen – 'You were really taking control of those hands of yours, how come they got away from you this time? What do you think you might do to keep them in check in a similar situation again?'

You could also do this with anger – 'How are these angry feelings getting the better of you? How can we stop this happening?'

For older students point out exceptions – when they do think before they act – as in tactical play in sport for instance.

Beware of reinforcing behavioural expectations by telling students what they can't do and labelling them.

⬤ Lying and denying responsibility

This may stem from a fear of consequences or because of a strong external locus of control. This is belief that things happen *to* you rather than being able to determine outcomes. This attributes success to luck rather than effort and failure to bad teaching rather than lack of work. 'It wasn't me' is infuriating but not worth an argument during class time. With a collaborative ethos you can focus on group responsibility with the individual being part of the group. You can say things like, 'Even if you didn't drop all the pencils we are all responsible for keeping everything in the right place. I will ask someone to help you pick them up.'

In the longer term an ethos where mistakes are considered to be part of learning helps. Be prepared to model this and admit that sometimes you get things wrong. You will not lose credibility. Comment regularly on students' responsibility for positive outcomes so they increase their sense of self-efficacy and internal locus of control.

⬤ High demands on your time and attention

Decide what gets minimal attention. Staying focused on the main issues gives students the message that you will not be distracted from your purpose in getting on with the teaching.

Some students try and take control by making you jump to their tune. Pupils who want you all the time or continually disrupt others are exhausting. They grind you down until responding to their demands seems the easier option. This, of course, reinforces behaviour you don't want and makes things much worse in the longer term.

Give strong and focused attention to the behaviours you do want. This means good eye contact, positive facial expression, positive and specific feedback. A system of rewards might be necessary in the first instance. Give disruptive behaviour minimal attention. If you have to intervene speak minimally, move the student away from others if necessary and keep a blank facial expression. A teacher made a badge for one student that said 'not now, Jason'. She kept this pinned to her and simply tapped it when he tried to gain attention at inappropriate times. She then chose when to respond and thanked him for waiting. (Roffey and O'Reirdan, 2003)

Students usually escalate attention seeking at first, so be prepared for this. It is essential to combine giving minimal attention for unwanted behaviour with strong positive attention for the wanted behaviour for the strategy to eventually work.

If a young student is having a tantrum because they are not getting their own way, you can train your class to also ignore it. This does work! Such tantrums are not an outburst of deep emotion but a strategy the pupil has learnt is rewarding. This could be anything from getting attention to sweets in a supermarket. You have to show this is not going to be successful with you. Put the control back to the student – 'Let me know when you want to join us again.' If the student is hurting herself or others you will need to intervene but do this with minimal fuss. The student will eventually realize that tantrums will not work with you and give them up.

Wind-ups

Some pupils – especially teenage students – will attempt to wind you up. It is a form of verbal bullying and teachers, as figures of authority, are seen as fair game. Pupils try and get under your skin about things that really matter to you. It is important you recognize what these are (see Chapter 2). Whether it is your height, weight, competence, religion, sexuality or accent, they will pick up on what gets you going. This taunting is also a way of testing out your reactions. Staying calm and 'going with the flow' is the best way of stopping it, especially if you can do so with a touch of humour and self-deprecation. If you get into a spin about it you will reinforce the behaviour. However unkind it is, find a way of letting it flow over you. Your ability to be laid back and not take yourself too seriously will raise your status and credibility.

Be prepared and think of appropriate dismissive phrases that 'go with the flow' and use humour to disarm. For example, for a verbal attack on weight – 'Yes. I'm booking two airline seats next time I fly', or a snide remark about sexual preference – 'I only give interviews to journalists who pay well'. Try doing this with a smile and you will find that the wind-ups melt away. Your status with the students also goes up as you demonstrate you are in control, do not take yourself too seriously and can join in with the joke. If wit does not come easily to you then work out some ready-made retorts for when situations arise.

● Students who can't, don't, won't, always and never!

It is tempting to talk in extreme ways about students who are challenging. Students who '*never* do as they are asked', who '*always* muck up', who 'haven't learnt *a thing*', and so on. Here a behaviourist model is useful as a basis for solution-focused interventions. Behaviourism deals only with what is observable both in actual behaviour and in the contexts it occurs.

It is helpful to know whether the student is actually unable to do what is asked or can but is refusing – 'can't' and 'won't' require different responses.

Reality check   What is actually going on? You can get an impression about behaviour that does not necessarily match what is happening.

Determine what the issue is. This means describing it in observable terms. Saying that a student is 'always disruptive' or 'never does as she is told' does not give a clear picture of what the student is actually doing. It is more useful to know 'Zara gets out of her seat 5 times an hour' or 'Winston shouted out in the class fifteen times on Wednesday'.

A solution-focused approach builds on the positive. 'Zara can stay in her seat for ten minutes.' 'Winston put his hand up to contribute to class 3 times on Wednesday.' It is often easier for students to learn or increase new behaviours than it is for them to reduce ones that are already established.

Traditionally the 'ABC' model identifies not only the problem behaviour (B) but also the antecedents (A) and consequences (C), to see what might be reinforcing the unwanted behaviour. You can also do that with exceptions. What are the circumstances when the student is behaving well, and what happens afterwards to reinforce this?

Once the behaviour has been selected do some observations and keep a tally. This gives you a baseline on which to evaluate improvements. You may find difficult behaviour occurs less often than you originally thought, or that it only happens after a break or when there is a writing activity. You may find the positive behaviour occurs when a student is with a particular friend or is given a more structured activity. This gives you things to build on and opportunities to structure and maximize success.

The chances are that the student who is causing you difficulties has several behaviours you would like to change. Don't worry about this; you only need target one or two. Choose what is either most open to change or underpins other behaviours. It is more difficult to change what is entrenched. Short-term gains set the spiral on an upward path and other behaviours often improve in a 'ripple effect' or 'virtuous cycle'.

Behavioural interventions – creating solutions

Build programs to increase positive behaviours that are incompatible with difficult behaviours. Ways of doing this depend on the ages of the students.

Discuss with the student the behaviour you would like them to develop, instead of the behaviour that is hard to manage. If they can identify a target themselves, all the better. Also discuss the reward system to be put in place. Students rarely change their behaviour out of the goodness of their hearts! Ensure the reward is something the student wants and is achievable. Targets should reflect where the student is currently at and build success from there.

The most valuable rewards for students of every age are positive letters home. Pupils want to please the people who are important to them and be seen as achieving in their eyes – you'd be amazed how even the toughest guy or coolest chick wants one of those letters. Check home circumstances first – if you decide that the student is unlikely to get the response they are looking for it could make matters worse. In that case a school-based reward would be better. Grade rewards so you build up to the big one – whatever it is. For example

Star charts   A student gets a star on a chart for each lesson or section of the day in which they behaved in the required way. A certain number of stars means a larger reward – perhaps a certificate. Several certificates lead to the big reward (Roffey and O'Reirdan, 2001).

Positive reports 'Going on report' is not uncommon in high schools. A student takes a report card around and teachers sign it at the end of each lesson if behaviour has been acceptable. This is usually seen as a sanction but it doesn't have to be. Negotiating personal and positive targets on these report cards works better.

In one secondary school a Year eight girl identified three things she would like to work on to stop her getting into trouble: having the right books and equipment with her, agreeing to work with the group she was assigned to and speaking to teachers politely. Politely was defined as 'not being lippy'! The deputy headteacher made a special report book on his computer that she then decorated. He checked out how she was doing regularly, firstly at the end of every day and then once a week. She did really well and was proud of herself. To the teacher's surprise several other students came and asked if they could have their own report book too. They had chosen to get positive attention for positive behaviour themselves!

Contracts An effective behaviour contract is negotiated between the student and the school. The student agrees to fulfil certain specified expectations such as completing homework on time. Teachers also have contractual obligations, such as giving positive feedback once a day. Expectations, rewards and penalties are clear to everyone. An imposed 'agreement' which is one-sided is not a contract and unlikely to be effective.

Challenging groups

One or two challenging students is one thing. A whole bunch of them is another.

The guidelines in Chapter 4 on you and your class will help in the first instance. The following are all worth a try.

- Look at what aspects of the situation are under your control and what is possible for you to change. You may need to pay more attention to aspects of your class management, such as the beginnings of activities.

- It is unlikely that all the students are equally challenging. Identify the most influential and establish a rapport with them.

- A whole class meeting or circle time may help. Focus initially on what is going well in the class and celebrate that. Then focus on what needs to change. Rogers (2000) suggests a questionnaire to all students prior to the meeting may be helpful.

- Discuss how people feel in this class. Work on how we all want to feel.

- Help students to problem solve and take responsibility. Ask them what they need from you to feel good about being in this class.

- Write decisions up and put them in a public place. Review and monitor how it is going regularly.

In a high school other teachers are likely to also be having a hard time with this class. Get collegial support that does not undermine you. An authoritarian teacher might walk into your class and stun them into silence by giving them a piece of her mind, but this does not help you, or any other teacher, after she has left.

PART D – YOUR OWN SURVIVAL

Maintaining personal and professional integrity

Some situations are intractable. Nothing seems to work. Your own need for survival is at its height. What you do now has implications for how you are seen by the rest of the class. It is assumed that you will have followed the guidance above.

Individual incidents

Remember your values and continue to use these as a foundation for your actions. Be respectful to the students and respectful to yourself. When you are congruent and consistent with your own beliefs you maintain personal and professional integrity and will be seen to be behaving with dignity. This gives you control of the situation even if the student is not responding. The following steps may be helpful.

- Acknowledge to the student and to yourself that you cannot 'make' anyone do anything.
- Show a belief in them and reframe their behaviour positively if possible.
- State what is happening that is unacceptable, ensuring that you refer to the behaviour only.
- Offer a face saving solution if possible.
- State the behaviour you want using an 'I' sentence, such as 'I need you to sit down and take part in this lesson.'
- Use a 'broken record' routine and repeat the previous statement up to three times with pauses for possible compliance.
- Stay calm and maintain self-control.
- If the student is not responding offer clear choices.
- Say the choice is theirs but all choices have outcomes and consequences.
- State the consequences attached to those choices – both positive and negative.
- The consequences for continuing unacceptable behaviour need to be enforceable – if not now, then later.
- Ask the student if he understands the choices he is making.
- Show concern for the student in wanting them to make 'good' choices for themselves.
- Pause.
- State choices and consequences again.
- Vacate the situation if it is safe to do so.
- State that you are giving the student space to think over the options.
- Continue with your teaching.

- State the choice the student has made.

- Ensure that you follow through with consequences. Other students will know and this impacts on their future behaviour.

This way of dealing with things promotes clarity in what is unacceptable, but also communicates respect and concern for the student. Importantly it maintains teacher control of the situation. Once you have gone through such a scenario you will be amazed at how strong you feel. Instead of feeling wrecked and helpless you will feel a sense of personal and professional well-being at having faced a tricky situation and handled it with integrity and a sense of agency.

Individual students

There are some children or young people who challenge you constantly, day after day. You may have a clear, consistent and caring program to improve the situation and it has had minimal impact. You are feeling demoralized and worn out. You may feel angry that this student is in your class and that you are expected to deal with their behaviour. Do what you can to maintain your emotional resources while acting professionally and with personal integrity at all times. Keep records so that you have evidence of everything you need to access support. Do not blame yourself; the tragedy of this young person's life is not your fault.

Getting back on track after the worst of days

You have had a terrible day where one or more of your students have been defiant, rude and possibly threatening. Someone may have tried to make you a laughing stock and you now feel not only the butt of someone's joke but that whole groups of students are making fun of you. You may have witnessed an individual being hostile to someone vulnerable. Perhaps you have not been in control of a situation and your failure seen by a colleague. Any of these things may have resulted in you feeling angry, defensive or despairing. You may be wondering whether you have had enough. It is going to take courage and the need to earn a living to go back into what now feels like the lion's den and face another day. You may start to feel that the only way for you to survive is to give as good as you get. Your thoughts turn to revenge!

Before you make any hasty decisions think over the following.

- Just about everyone who is reading this book will have had at least one experience when they feel like you do now, including the author. You are not alone!

- Use your own desperation to understand how your most challenging students may feel. Many will have experienced rejection, abuse, failure, loss or neglect. If really bad days can cause you to feel this upset imagine what it must be like to be regularly abused at the hands of those who are supposed to care for you. It may help give you the motivation, and some insights, to work with these students rather than against them.

- You have choices. So do your students, but they are not the same choices and in many circumstances they are fewer. Tighter and tighter control and the exercise of power are more likely to exacerbate the situation. Clarity and consistency in expectations along with fairness and choice will raise the possibility of more positive outcomes.

- Personal preservation requires a holistic approach. You need to maximize your emotional strength to do what is optimal in the classroom. This will enable you to maintain your personal integrity even at the most challenging times.

- Tomorrow is another day – for you and for your students. Although our personal histories are integral to our expectations and the way we respond, these do not bind us. The incremental differences we develop in our classroom practice eventually add up to a whole new experience. Every mistake is a learning opportunity. Don't forget that if you are embarking on a consistent new way of being it takes time for others to have different expectations. Don't expect changes overnight.

SUMMARY

This chapter has addressed your biggest challenges: not just students and situations, but also challenges to the way you think, how you build relationships and the best ways to survive. It is stressed that the strategies here are just part of the whole picture. These need an optimal context to ensure their effectiveness. Believe in yourself. The ultimate aim is not just your survival but also the ability to thrive as a teacher and love what you are doing. This will make a great difference, not only to your own life but also the lives of your students. You may never know how much.

Chapter 8

Summary and Useful Reading

A brief overview of things to try, and what to avoid.

YOU PERSONALLY

Do

- look after yourself
- cherish your nurturing relationships
- be honest with yourself about where your time goes
- plan time flexibly
- find time to exercise – even walking is better than nothing
- relax with things you love to do
- learn to look confident
- know what your emotional triggers are
- pay attention to your emotional resources
- keep things in perspective
- spend some time reflecting on your beliefs, values, motivations and world-view
- keep your sense of humour
- be squeaky clean!

Don't

- give up because of one bad day – or even a bad week
- take too much notice of the negative voices in your head – keep them under control
- take yourself too seriously
- let your emotions dictate your reactions – think them through.

IN SCHOOL AND IN THE COMMUNITY

Do

- look for where your support lies
- know who to ask for practical help and guidance
- learn from respected colleagues
- have solution-focused discussions
- check out the relevant policies
- learn about the communities the school serves
- understand parents have a role to play
- remind yourself that most parents do the best they can with the skills, knowledge, resources and support available to them
- reflect on your own prejudices.

Don't

- spend too much time with colleagues who are immersed in negativity
- present parents with lists of student misdemeanours
- pre-judge people.

IN YOUR CLASS

Do

- be in charge

- be well prepared and on time for lessons

- link material to student interest

- have good pace and variety in your delivery

- teach routines and expectations

- find effective ways of getting attention

- encourage and facilitate self-control

- give students input and choices

- encourage problem-solving

- work on developing a supportive class ethos

- teach students both collaborative skills and how to work independently

- take account of different learning abilities

- structure success experience

- ask rather than demand

- listen as well as talk

- be aware of your voice – volume, tenor and pitch

- have high but realistic expectations

- move around the room, be aware of interactions

- pre-empt and prevent disruption.

Don't

- be controlling

- focus on punishment

- set children up to fail
- have favourites
- stand with your back to students
- back pupils into no-win situations.

PROMOTING THE BEHAVIOUR YOU WANT

Do

- be clear about what you expect
- walk the talk – model what you expect
- develop a short list of class rules with students
- have rules that begin with 'do' rather than 'don't'
- focus on what you *want* the students to do rather than what they are doing
- give attention to the behaviours you want
- pay attention to the beginnings and endings of lessons and activities
- give reminders before reprimands
- have positive expectations and give positive labels
- provide incentives
- address constructive criticism to groups rather than individuals where possible.

Don't

- be dictatorial
- keep talking about what students are not doing or doing badly.

DEVELOPING GOOD RELATIONSHIPS

Do

- smile
- be interested in students as people
- listen – at appropriate times
- acknowledge strengths and qualities
- emphasize personal bests rather than comparing with others
- find something to like
- be friendly – but not a friend
- use 'I' statements.

Don't

- be inconsistent and moody
- belittle or use put-downs as a means of management
- get into arguments
- shout down.

DEALING WITH CHALLENGING BEHAVIOUR

Do

- refer to the behaviour as unacceptable not to the student
- check on learning needs
- avoid negative labels
- look for strengths and exceptions
- take account of the emotional context
- frame behaviour into what is meaningful for the student
- acknowledge the feelings of the student
- aim for win-win outcomes

- give face saving solutions
- use non-threatening body language
- keep your voice low and slow
- offer consequences as a choice
- ensure consequences are realistic
- give time for compliance
- always follow up situations
- use short term management strategies that are congruent with longer term interventions.

Don't

- jump to conclusions
- make assumptions
- attribute blame
- take things personally
- mirror anger
- try and 'make' someone do something
- interrogate.

Do say to students

- What do you need?
- How can I help?
- Well done for . . .
- I am proud of you because . . .
- I like the way you . . .
- We all make mistakes.
- What could you do to make it better?
- What do you think should happen now?

- I'll just give you a few minutes . . .

- I'm sorry, I don't think I got that right/understood properly.

- Tomorrow is another day.

- I can see you are upset but (behaving like this) is not acceptable in this class.

- How can you say this so I can really hear you?

Don't say to students

- Why do you never/always . . .

- Why can't you . . .

- Of course it's not difficult.

- How many times do I have to tell you?

- I'm going to make you . . .

- You're not the only one in this class.

- You are nothing but . . .

- Why can't you always be like this?

- You are just over-reacting.

A BRIEF LIST OF REALLY USEFUL RESOURCES

The References section gives details along with other relevant sources.

Schools

High Risk Children in Schools (1996) by Robert Pianta and Daniel Walsh uses an eco-systemic analysis in relation to constructing relationships in schools for vulnerable children.

In *Developing the Emotionally Literate School* (2004) Katherine Weare shows clearly how emotional issues impact at every level of the system. The chapter, 'What Kind of Schools Promote Emotional Literacy' is relevant here.

Antidote's *The Emotional Literacy Handbook* (2003) shows how this can be developed at a whole school level.

Gerdo Hanko's book *Increasing Competence though Collaborative Problem-Solving* (1999) illustrates how teachers can positively support each other.

Louise Stoll and Dean Fink look at the power of school culture and possibilities for change in *Changing our Schools* (1995).

Promoting a positive classroom climate

Bill Rogers has written widely on behaviour management with ideas that often mirror those here. In *Classroom Behaviour* (2000) he also refers to Kounin's *Discipline and Group Management in Classrooms* (1971).

Michelle MacGrath in *The Art of Teaching Peacefully* (1998) has an excellent chapter on developing relationships with your class and another on managing stress and cultivating calm.

Circle of Friends (Newton and Wilson, 1999) outlines an intervention in which the needs of marginalized students are addressed by a group of volunteer peers.

Circle time

There are now numerous books on circle time. Jenny Mosley has written many of them such as *Turn Your School Around* (1993), and *Quality Circle Time in the Primary School* (1996). Lucky Duck publishes several others.

ELECT provides consultancy and training internationally on social, emotional and behavioural issues in schools and also circle time in Australia. Contact mail@elect-consultants.com.

Conflict resolution

Everyone Can Win (1989) by Helena Cornelius and Shoshana Faire is a classic. It covers all the main elements of conflict and cooperation, power, assertiveness, mediation, negotiation and empathy.

A detailed outline of peer mediation in schools has been written by Richard Cohen entitled *Students Resolving Conflict* (1995).

Developing social and emotional literacy

An excellent introductory book on systemic development in emotional literacy is Peter Sharp's *Nurturing Emotional Literacy* (2001).

For individual skills Carolyn Webster-Stratton's *How to Promote Children's Emotional and Social Competence* (1999) is excellent.

Teaching Social Behaviour by David Warden and Donald Christie (1997) is also full of practical ideas.

Solution-focused thinking

Solutions in Schools, edited by Yasmin Ajmal and Ioan Rees, covers a range of both pro-active and reactive issues in schools, presenting a solution-focused approach for each.

Other authors to look out for are Steve de Shazer, Chris Iveson and colleagues, Michael Durrant, Bill O'Hanlon, Michael White and Insoo Kim Berg.

Parents and the community

Andy Miller's *Teachers, Parents and Classroom Behaviour* (2003) builds on his earlier work *Pupil Behaviour and Teacher Culture* (1996).

School Behaviour and Families covers a range of issues faced by teachers at the home–school interface and ways of addressing them (Roffey, 2002).

Addressing specific behaviours

Bill Roger's *Cracking the Hard Class* (1997) is well worth reading.

Faber and Mazlish's *How to Talk so Kids will Listen and How to Listen so Kids will Talk* was first published in 1980. Although intended for families it has much that is applicable in school. It uses cartoons to illustrate how ways of speaking to children and young people – such as using 'I' statements – make a huge difference.

Sue Roffey and Terry O'Reirdan wrote *Plans for Better Behaviour in the Primary School* (2003) on the basis of work done with groups of teachers, educational psychologists and support staff. They identify a range of specific behaviours that primary classroom teachers find difficult, summarize ways of managing and provide ideas about what might be done to change behaviour in the longer term.

The bigger picture

Tom Billington's *Separating, Losing and Excluding Children* (2000) is an account of the critical psychology perspective if you want to get into the theory behind the thinking.

For an illustration of how young people might come to be misread and marginalized read *The Wrong Boy* (2000) by Willy Russell. Although a fictional work, the experiences that are described mirror what happens for some young people.

References

Admiraal, W.F., Korthagen, F.A.J. and Wubbels, L. (2000) 'Effects of student teachers' coping'. *British Journal of Educational Psychology*, 70: 33–41.

Ajmal, Y. and Rees, I. (eds) (2001) *Solutions in Schools: Creative Applications of Solution Focused Brief Thinking with Young People and Adults*. London: BT Press.

Anguiano, P. (2001) 'A first-year teacher's plan to reduce misbehaviour in the classroom'. *Teaching Exceptional Children*, 33: 52–55.

Antidote (2003) *The Emotional Literacy Handbook: Promoting Whole-School Strategies*. London: David Fulton Publishers.

Appl, D.J., Troha, C. and Rowell, J. (2001) 'Reflections of a first year team: The growth of a collaborative partnership'. *Teaching Exceptional Children*, 33: 4–8.

Assor, A., Kaplan, H. and Roth, G. (2002) 'Choice is good, but relevance is excellent: Autonomy-enhancing and suppressing teacher behaviours predicting students' engagement in schoolwork'. *British Journal of Educational Psychology*, 72: 261–278.

Barnett, K. and McCormick, J. (2003) 'Vision, relationships and teacher motivation: A case study'. *Journal of Educational Administration*, 41.1: 55.

Baumrind, D. (1971) 'Current patterns of parental authority'. *Developmental Psychology Monograph 4* (No.1 Pt 2).

Baumrind, D. (1991) 'The influence of parenting style on adolescent competence and substance abuse'. *Journal of Early Adolescence*, 11: 56–95.

Beishuizen, J.J., Hof, E., Van Putten, C.M., Bouwmeester, S. and Asscher, J.J. (2001) 'Students' and teachers' cognitions about good teachers'. *British Journal of Educational Psychology*, 71: 185–190.

Berg, I.K. and Steiner, T. (2003) *Children's Solution Work*. New York, London: W.W.Norton.

Bibou-Nakou, G., Kiosseoglou, G. and Stogiannidou, A. (2000) 'Elementary teachers perceptions regarding school behaviour problems: Implications for school psychological services'. *Psychology in the Schools,* 37(2): 123–133.

Billington, T. (2000) *Separating, Losing and Excluding Children: Narratives of Difference.* London, New York: Routledge Falmer.

Black, R. (1987) *Getting Things Done.* London: Douglas Petersen.

Blake, D., Hanley, V., Jennings, M., and Lloyd. M. (2000) 'Superteachers: The views of teachers and head teachers on the advanced skills teacher grade'. *Research in Education,* 63: 48–53.

Blanton, P. (2002) 'Classroom climate'. *The Physics Teacher,* 40: 50–51.

Bobek, B.L. (2002) 'Teacher Resiliency: A key to career longevity'. *The Clearing House,* 75: 202–205.

Boich, G. (1995) *Becoming a Teacher: An Inquiring Dialogue for the Beginner Teacher.* London: The Falmer Press.

Brighouse, T. (2000) 'How some schools stretch success to new levels', presentation at Service Children's Education Conference in Loccum, Germany, 25 October 2000. Cited in Sharp, P. (2001) *Nurturing Emotional Literacy.* London: David Fulton Publishers.

Brighton, C.M. (1999) 'Keeping good teachers: Lessons from novices', in Scherer, M. (ed) *A Better Beginning: Supporting and Mentoring New Teachers.* Alexandria: Association for Supervision and Curriculum Development.

Bronfennbrenner, U. (1979) *The Ecology of Human Development: Experiments by Nature and Design.* Cambridge, Mass and London: Harvard University Press.

Brophy, J. (1996) 'Enhancing students' socialisation: Key elements: ERIC digest'. *ERIC Clearinghouse on Elementary and Early Childhood Education.* Illinois, USA: ERIC.

Cains, R.A. and Brown, C.R. (1998) 'Newly qualified teachers: A comparative analysis of the perceptions held by B.Ed and PGCE trained primary teachers on the level and frequency of stress experienced during the first year of teaching'. *Educational Psychology,* 18: 97–110.

Cameron, R. (2001) 'Identifying the developmental phases encountered by beginning teachers during an internship', in Jeffrey, P. (ed) *Conference of the Australian Association for Research in Education.* Melbourne: Australian Association for Research in Education.

Canter, L. and Canter, M. (1976) *Assertive Discipline: A Take Charge Approach for Today's Educator.* California: Canter and Associates.

Cantor, D. and Wright, M. (2002) 'School crime patterns: A national profile of US public high schools using rates of crime reported to police', in *Report of the Study of School Violence and Prevention*. Washington DC: Department of Education.

Cohen, R. (1995) *Students Resolving Conflict*. Illinois, USA: Good Year Books.

Comerford, D. and Jacobson, M. (1987) *Capital Punishment for Misdemeanours*. Paper presented at the American Educational Research Association, Washington DC: April 20–24.

Commonwealth Department of Education, Science and Training (2002) *An Ethic of Care: Effective Programmes for Beginning Teachers*. Canberra: Australian Government Publications Service.

Cornelius, H. and Faire, S. (1989) *Everyone Can Win: How to Resolve Conflict*. East Roseville, NSW: Simon and Schuster.

Costigan, A. (2002) 'Teaching the culture of high stakes testing: Listening to new teachers'. *Action in Teacher Education*, Winter Edition: 28–34.

Cullen, K. and Ramoutar, L. (2003) 'Building fresh perceptions of a class: Turning "horrors" into "lovelies" '. *Educational and Child Psychology*, 20.4: 116–130.

Currie, W. (2003) 'Teacher Supply Reaching Crisis'. *Education*, 1 September: 5.

Day, C. and Leitch, R. (2001) 'Teacher and teacher educators' lives: the role of emotion'. *Teaching and Teacher Education*, 17: 403–415.

Dearden, J. (1994) 'Support at the primary level', in Gray, P., Miller, A. and Noakes, J. *Challenging Behaviour in Schools*. London: Routledge.

Department for Education and Skills (1989) *Discipline in Schools (The Elton Report)*. London: HMSO.

Department for Education and Skills (2003) www.teachernet.gov.uk.

Diniz, F. (2002) 'Working with families in multi-ethnic European context: implication for services', in Carpenter, B. (ed) *Families in Context*. London: David Fulton Publishers.

Dockrell, J. and Lindsay, G. (2000) 'The behaviour and self-esteem of children with specific speech and language difficulties'. *British Journal of Educational Psychology*, 70: 4.

Dorman, J.P., Fraser, B.J. and McRobbie, C. (1997) 'Relationship between school-level and classroom-level environments in secondary schools'. *Journal of Educational Administration*, 35: 74–91.

Dowling, E. and Gorell Barnes, G. (2000) *Working with Children and Parents through Separation and Divorce*. Basingstoke: Macmillan Press.

Doyle, R. (2003) 'Developing the nurturing school'. *Emotional and Behavioural Difficulties*, 8.4: 252–266.

Elliott, J. (2004) 'Educational Psychologists and Problem Behaviour in Schools', keynote speech at the British Psychological Society Division of Educational and Child Psychology conference, Paris, 7 January 2004.

Ewing, R. (2001) 'Keeping beginning teachers in the profession'. *Independent Education*, 31(3): 30–32.

Faber, A. and Mazlish, E. (1980) *How to Talk so Kids will Listen and How to Listen so Kids will Talk*. New York: Avon Books.

Faupel, A., Herrick, E. and Sharp P. (1998) *Anger Management: A Practical Guide*. London: David Fulton Publishers.

Friedman, I. (2003) 'Self-efficacy and burnout in teaching: The importance of interpersonal relations efficacy'. *Social Psychology of Education*, 6(3): 191–215.

Fuller, A. (1998) *From Surviving to Thriving: Promoting Mental Health in Young People*. Victoria: Australian Council for Educational Research.

Galus, P. (2002) 'All I need to know about teaching I learnt from my students'. *The Physics Teacher*, 40: 557–558.

Gamman, R. (2003) 'Sharing the load, supporting the staff: Collaborative management of difficult behaviour in primary schools'. *Emotional and Behavioural Difficulties*, 8(3): 217–229.

Goleman, D. and the Dalai Lama (2003) *Destructive Emotions: How Can We Overcome Them?* New York: Bantam Books.

Goleman, D. (1995) *Emotional Intelligence: Why It Can Matter More Than IQ*. London: Bloomsbury.

Greenfield, S. (2000) *The Private Life of the Brain*. London: Penguin Press.

Grote, M. (1995) 'Sure you care, but do students know it?' *The Physics Teacher*, 33: 92–95.

Hall, E., Hall, C. and Abaci, R. (1997) 'The effects of human relationships training on reported teacher stress, pupil control ideology and locus of control'. *British Journal of Educational Psychology*, 67: 483–496.

Hanko, G. (1999) *Increasing Competence through Collaborative Problem-Solving*. London: David Fulton Publishers.

Hargeaves, A. (1994) *Changing Teachers, Changing Times: Teachers' Work and Culture in the Postmodern Age*. London: Cassell.

Haroun, R. and O'Hanlon, C. (1997) 'Do teachers and students agree in their perceptions of what school discipline is?' *Educational Psychology Review*, 49: 234–250.

Harre, R. and Parrott, W. (1996) *The Emotions: Social, Cultural and Biological Dimensions.* London: Sage Publishers.

Harskamp, A. (2002) 'Working with parents who harm their children' in Roffey, S. (ed) *School Behaviour and Families,* London: David Fulton Publishers.

Hastings, R. and Bham, M. (2003) 'The relationship between student behaviour patterns and teacher burnout'. *School Psychology International,* 24(1): 115–128.

Hay McBer (2000) *Research into Teacher Effectiveness: A model of teacher effectiveness.* Research Report No 216. Norwich: HMSO.

Hertzog, H.S. (2002) ' "When, how and who do I ask for help?" Novices' perceptions of problems and assistance'. *Teacher Education Quarterly,* 29: 25–41.

Honan, E., Knobel, M., Baker, C. and Davies, B. (1998) 'The accomplishment of good studenthood: Multiple readings'. Cited in Laws, C. and Davies, B. (2000) 'Post structuralist theory in practice: working with "behaviourally disturbed" children'. *International Journal of Qualitative Studies in Education,* 13(3): 205–221.

Huberman, M. (1993) *The Lives of Teachers.* London: Cassell.

Kaplan, A., Gheen. M. and Midgley, C. (2002) 'Classroom goal structure and student disruptive behaviour'. *British Journal of Educational Psychology,* 72: 191–211.

Keating, J.E. (2000) 'Keeping the Teaching on Track'. *Instructor,* 110: 27–28.

Kellerman, K. and Shea, B. (1996) 'Threats, suggestions, hints and promises: Gaining compliance efficiently and politely'. *Communication quarterly,* 44 (2): 145–166.

Kounin, J. (1971) *Discipline and Group Management in Classrooms.* New York: Holt Rheinhart and Winston.

Jaffe, P., Wolfe, D., Wilson, S. and Zak, L. (1986) 'Family violence and child adjustment: A comparative analysis of girls' and boys' behavioural symptoms'. *American Journal of Orthopsychiatry,* 143(1): 73–76.

Jules, V. and Kutnick, P. (1997) 'Student perceptions of a good teacher. The gender perspective'. *British Journal of Educational Psychology,* 67: 497–511.

Laird, J. and Apostoleris, N. (1996) 'Emotional self-control and self-perception: Feelings are the solution, not the problem' in Harre, R. and Parrott, W. (1996) *The Emotions: Social, Cultural and Biological Dimensions.* London: Sage Publications.

Larivee, B. (2002) 'The potential perils of praise in a democratic interactive classroom'. *Action in Teacher Education*, 23: 77–88.

Laws, C. and Davies, B. (2000) 'Post structuralist theory in practice: working with "behaviourally disturbed" children'. *International Journal of Qualitative Studies in Education*, 13(3): 205–221.

Lieberman, A. (ed) (1988) *Building a Professional Culture in Schools*. New York: Teachers College Press.

Lockwood, J. (1995) 'From nightmare to dream'. *The Journal of the Astronomical Society of the Pacific*, 24: 10.

Manuel, J. (2002) 'A teacher of excellence: experiences of beginning teachers'. *Education Links*, 65: 32–36.

MacGrath, M. (1998) *The Art of Teaching Peacefully*. London: David Fulton Publishers.

Marsh, C. (2000) *Handbook for Beginning Teachers* (2nd edition). French's Forest: Longman.

Mastrilli, T. and Sardo-Brown, D. (2002) 'Novice teachers' cases: A vehicle for reflective practice'. *Education*, 123: 56–62.

McLaughlin, M.W. and Talbert, J.W. (1993) *Contexts that Matter for Teaching and Learning*. Palo Alto, CA: Center for Research on the Context of Secondary School Teaching.

McNally J.G. (1994) 'Students, schools and a matter of mentors'. *The International Journal of Education Management*, 8(5): 18–20.

Michael, R. (ed) (1987) 'Educating emotionally disturbed children – promising practices. Journal within a journal'. *Perceptions*, 23:1.

Miller, A., Ferguson, E. and Moore, E. (2002) 'Parents' and pupils' causal attributions for difficult classroom behaviour'. *British Journal of Educational Psychology*, 72: 27–31.

Miller, A. (1996) *Pupil Behaviour and Teacher Culture*. London: Cassell.

Miller, A. (2003) *Teachers, Parents and Classroom Behaviour: A Psychosocial Approach*. Maidenhead: Open University Press.

Milner, H. (2001) 'A qualitative investigation of teachers' planning and efficacy for student engagement'. *Dissertation Abstracts International Section A: Humanities and Social Sciences*, 62: 1315.

Morehead, M.A. (1998) 'Professional behaviours for the beginning teacher'. *American Secondary Education*, 26: 22–27.

Mosley, J. (1993) *Turn Your School Round*. Cambridgeshire: Cambs LDA.

References

Admiraal, W.F., Korthagen, F.A.J. and Wubbels, L. (2000) 'Effects of student teachers' coping'. *British Journal of Educational Psychology*, 70: 33–41.

Ajmal, Y. and Rees, I. (eds) (2001) *Solutions in Schools: Creative Applications of Solution Focused Brief Thinking with Young People and Adults*. London: BT Press.

Anguiano, P. (2001) 'A first-year teacher's plan to reduce misbehaviour in the classroom'. *Teaching Exceptional Children*, 33: 52–55.

Antidote (2003) *The Emotional Literacy Handbook: Promoting Whole-School Strategies*. London: David Fulton Publishers.

Appl, D.J., Troha, C. and Rowell, J. (2001) 'Reflections of a first year team: The growth of a collaborative partnership'. *Teaching Exceptional Children*, 33: 4–8.

Assor, A., Kaplan, H. and Roth, G. (2002) 'Choice is good, but relevance is excellent: Autonomy-enhancing and suppressing teacher behaviours predicting students' engagement in schoolwork'. *British Journal of Educational Psychology*, 72: 261–278.

Barnett, K. and McCormick, J. (2003) 'Vision, relationships and teacher motivation: A case study'. *Journal of Educational Administration*, 41.1: 55.

Baumrind, D. (1971) 'Current patterns of parental authority'. *Developmental Psychology Monograph 4* (No.1 Pt 2).

Baumrind, D. (1991) 'The influence of parenting style on adolescent competence and substance abuse'. *Journal of Early Adolescence*, 11: 56–95.

Beishuizen, J.J., Hof, E., Van Putten, C.M., Bouwmeester, S. and Asscher, J.J. (2001) 'Students' and teachers' cognitions about good teachers'. *British Journal of Educational Psychology*, 71: 185–190.

Berg, I.K. and Steiner, T. (2003) *Children's Solution Work*. New York, London: W.W.Norton.

Bibou-Nakou, G., Kiosseoglou, G. and Stogiannidou, A. (2000) 'Elementary teachers perceptions regarding school behaviour problems: Implications for school psychological services'. *Psychology in the Schools*, 37(2): 123–133.

Billington, T. (2000) *Separating, Losing and Excluding Children: Narratives of Difference*. London, New York: Routledge Falmer.

Black, R. (1987) *Getting Things Done*. London: Douglas Petersen.

Blake, D., Hanley, V., Jennings, M., and Lloyd. M. (2000) 'Superteachers: The views of teachers and head teachers on the advanced skills teacher grade'. *Research in Education*, 63: 48–53.

Blanton, P. (2002) 'Classroom climate'. *The Physics Teacher*, 40: 50–51.

Bobek, B.L. (2002) 'Teacher Resiliency: A key to career longevity'. *The Clearing House*, 75: 202–205.

Boich, G. (1995) *Becoming a Teacher: An Inquiring Dialogue for the Beginner Teacher*. London: The Falmer Press.

Brighouse, T. (2000) 'How some schools stretch success to new levels', presentation at Service Children's Education Conference in Loccum, Germany, 25 October 2000. Cited in Sharp, P. (2001) *Nurturing Emotional Literacy*. London: David Fulton Publishers.

Brighton, C.M. (1999) 'Keeping good teachers: Lessons from novices', in Scherer, M. (ed) *A Better Beginning: Supporting and Mentoring New Teachers*. Alexandria: Association for Supervision and Curriculum Development.

Bronfennbrenner, U. (1979) *The Ecology of Human Development: Experiments by Nature and Design*. Cambridge, Mass and London: Harvard University Press.

Brophy, J. (1996) 'Enhancing students' socialisation: Key elements: ERIC digest'. *ERIC Clearinghouse on Elementary and Early Childhood Education*. Illinois, USA: ERIC.

Cains, R.A. and Brown, C.R. (1998) 'Newly qualified teachers: A comparative analysis of the perceptions held by B.Ed and PGCE trained primary teachers on the level and frequency of stress experienced during the first year of teaching'. *Educational Psychology*, 18: 97–110.

Cameron, R. (2001) 'Identifying the developmental phases encountered by beginning teachers during an internship', in Jeffrey, P. (ed) *Conference of the Australian Association for Research in Education*. Melbourne: Australian Association for Research in Education.

Canter, L. and Canter, M. (1976) *Assertive Discipline: A Take Charge Approach for Today's Educator*. California: Canter and Associates.

Mosley, J. (1996) *Quality Circle Time in the Primary School.* Cambridgeshire: Cambs LDA.

Moss, H. and Wilson V. (1998) 'Using Circle Time in a Primary School'. *Pastoral Care*, September.

Newton, D.P. and Newton, L.D. (2001) 'Choosing and judging teachers: What heads and student teachers think matters'. *The Journal of Education for Teaching*, 25: 135–150.

Newton, C. and Wilson, D. (1999) *Circle of Friends.* Dunstable: Folens Publishers.

NSW Department of Education and Training (2001) *Induction for Teachers.* Sydney: Training and Development Directorate.

NSW Public Education Inquiry (2001) *Final Reports Third Report 55 Ch. 11 Guidance during the first professional years.* Sydney: NSW Department of Education and Training.

Oberski, I., Ford, K., Higgins, S. and Fisher, P. (1999) 'The importance of relationships in teacher education'. *Journal of Education for Teaching*, 25(2): 135–150.

Oosterheert, I., Vermunt, J. and Denessen, E. (2002) 'Assessing orientations to learning to teach'. *The British Journal of Educational Psychology*, March 2002.

Patterson, N.C., Roehrig, G.H. and Luft. J.A. (2003) 'Running the treadmill: Explorations of beginning high school science teacher turnover in Arizona'. *The High School Journal*, 86: 14–22.

Pellegrini, A and Blatchford, P. (2000) *The Child at School: Interactions with Peers and Teachers.* London: Edward Arnold.

Pianta, R.C. and Walsh, D.J. (1996) *High Risk Children in Schools: Constructing Sustaining Relationships.* New York: Routledge.

Preston, D. (2000) *Teacher Supply and Demand to 2005.* Canberra: Australian Council of Deans of Education.

Public Education Inquiry NSW (2001) *Guidance during the first professional years.* http://www.pub-ed-inquiry.org/reports/final reports/04/Ch11.

Ramsey, G. (2000) *Quality matters: Revitalising teaching: Critical times, critical choices.* Sydney: NSW Department of Education and Training.

Renard, L. (1999) 'Ask not what your school can do for you but what you can do for your school', in Scherer, M. (ed) *A Better Beginning: Supporting and Mentoring New Teachers.* Alexandria: Association for Supervision and Curriculum Development.

Robinson, W.P. and Taylor, C.A. (1999) 'An evaluation of a circle time programme for Year 7 pupils', University of Bristol unpublished report, cited in Antidote (2003) *The Emotional Literacy Handbook*. London: David Fulton Publishers.

Roffey, S. (ed) (2002) *School Behaviour and Families: Frameworks for Working Together*. London: David Fulton Publishers.

Roffey, S. and O'Reirdan, T. (2001) *Young Children and Classroom Behaviour: Needs, Perspectives and Strategies*. London: David Fulton Publishers.

Roffey, S. and O'Reirdan, T. (2003) *Plans for Better Behaviour in the Primary School: Management and Intervention*. London: David Fulton Publishers.

Roffey, S., Tarrant, T. and Majors, K. (1994) *Young Friends, Schools and Friendship*. London: Cassell Education.

Roffey, S., Asfoura, L., Bayliss, B., Dilek, J., Graeme-Holder, R. and Sims, D. (2004) *New Teachers, Relationships and Behaviour*. Sydney: University of Western Sydney (work in progress).

Rogers, B. (1997) *Cracking the Hard Class: Strategies for Managing the Harder than Average Class*. London: Paul Chapman Publishing.

Rogers, B. (2000) *Classroom Behaviour: A Practical Guide to Effective Teaching, Behaviour Management and Colleague Support*. London: Books Education.

Rose, M.C. (2000) 'All together now! Creating a positive classroom from day one'. *Instructor*, 110: 22.

Russell, W. (2000) *The Wrong Boy*. London: Doubleday.

Rutter, J. (1994) *Working with Refugee Children in the Classroom*. Stoke on Trent: Trentham Books.

Rutter, M. and Maughan, B. (2002) 'School Effectiveness Findings 1979–2002'. *Journal of School Psychology*, 40(6): 451–475.

Santora, N. (1999) 'Relationships of power: An analysis of school practicum discourse'. *Journal of Intercultural Studies*, 20: 1–10.

Schutz, P.A., Crowder, K.C. and White, V.E. (2001) 'The development of a goal to become a teacher'. *Journal of Educational Psychology*, 93: 299–308.

Sharp, P. (2001) *Nurturing Emotional Literacy*. London: David Fulton Publishers.

Sharp, S. and Smith, P.K. (1994) *School Bullying: Insights and Perspectives*. London: Routledge.

Smith, A. (1998) *Accelerated Learning in Practice*. Buckinghamshire: Alite Ltd.

Smithers, A. and Robinson, P. (2003) *Factors Affecting Teachers' Decisions to Leave the Profession*. DfES Research Report RR430: University of Liverpool.

Steinberg, L., Lamborn, S., Darling, N., Mounts, N. and Dornbusch, S. (1994) 'Over-time adjustments and competence in adolescents from authoritative, authoritarian, indulgent and neglectful families'. *Child Development*, 57: 841–851.

Stephenson, J., Linfoot, K. and Martin, A. (2000) 'Behaviours of concern to teachers in the early years of school'. *International Journal of Disability, Development and Education*, 47(3): 225–235.

Sternberg, K., Lamb, M., Greenbaum C., Cicchetti, D., Dawud, S., Cortes, M., Krispin, O. and Lorey, F. (1993) 'Effects of domestic violence on children's behaviour problems and depression'. *Developmental Psychology*, 29(1): 44–52.

Stoel, C.F. and Thant, T.S. (2002) *Teachers Professional Lives: A View from Nine Industrialised Countries*. Washington, DC: Milken Family Foundation.

Stoll, L. and Fink, D. (1995) *Changing Our Schools*. Buckingham: Open University Press.

Stuhlman, M. and Pianta, R. (2002) 'Teachers narratives about their relationships with children: Associations with behaviour in classrooms'. *School Psychology Review*, 31(2): 148–151.

Teachernet (2003) *Managing Behaviour in your classroom*. http://www.teachernet.gov.uk/professionaldevelopment/opportunities/behaviourmanagement/classroombehaviour/

Teachernet (2003) *Taking the heat out of the moment*. http://www.teachernet.gov.uk/professionaldevelopment/opportunities/nqt/behaviourtips/

Tirri, K. (1999) 'Teachers' perceptions of moral dilemmas at school'. *Journal of Moral Education*, 28: 31–47.

Turner, J.C., Meyer, D.K., Midgley, C. and Patrick, H. (2003) 'Teacher discourse and sixth graders' reported affect and achievement behaviours in two high mastery/high performance mathematics classroom's'. *The Elementary School Journal*, 103: 357–382.

Wadsworth, D. (2001) 'Why new teachers choose to teach'. *Educational Leadership*, 58(8): 24–28.

Warden, D. and Christie, D. (1997) *Teaching Social Behaviour: Classroom Activities to Foster Children's Interpersonal Awareness*. London: David Fulton Publishers.

Weare, K. (2003) *What Works in Developing Children's Social and Emotional Competence and Wellbeing?* Report for the Department of Education and Skills: University of Southampton.

Weare, K. (2004) *Developing the Emotionally Literate School*. London: Paul Chapman Publishing.

Webster-Stratton, C. (1999) *How to Promote Children's Emotional and Social Competence*. London: Paul Chapman Publishing.

Weinstein, C.S. (1998) ' "I want to be nice, but I have to be mean": Exploring prospective teachers' conceptions of caring and order'. *Teaching and Teacher Education,* 14(2): 153–163.

Weiss, S. (2002) 'How teachers' autobiographies influence their responses to children's behaviours: The psychodynamic concept of transference in classroom life'. *Emotional and Behavioural Difficulties,* 7(2): 109–127.

Williams, A. and Prestage, S. (2001) 'Teacher culture and the induction of newly qualified teachers', in Jeffrey, P.L. (ed) *Conference of the Australian Association for Research in Education 2001.* Melbourne: Australian Association for Research in Education.

Winslade, J. and Monk, G. (1999) *Narrative Counselling in Schools.* Thousand Oaks: Corwin Press.

Wormington, A. (2002) 'Working with mobile families', in Roffey, S. (ed) *School Behaviour and Families.* London: David Fulton Publishers.

Worsham, M. and Emmer, E. (1983) *Teachers Planning Decisions for the Beginning of School.* Texas University: Research and Development Centre for Teacher Education.

Worthy, J. (2001) ' "I can't wait to see Carlos!": Pre-service teachers, situated learning, and personal relationships with students'. *Journal of Literacy Research,* June 2001.

Index